RAZED BY TV SETS

Jason McCall

autofocus books
Orlando, Florida

©Jason McCall, 2024
All rights reserved.

Published by Autofocus Books
autofocuslit.com

Essay/Literature
ISBN: 978-1-957392-28-8

Cover Illustration ©Amy Wheaton
Library of Congress Control Number: 2023951479

RAZED BY TV SETS

*For the people who taught me
how to love every version of me.*

Table of Contents

Scoot Back. You're Hurting Your Eyes.

My Dad Still Watches the NFL..9

We Hate *Wonder Woman 1984* Because
Nobody Ever Granted Our Wish..15

Watching Tennis Is the Whitest Thing
I'll Ever Be Allowed To Do..17

Tha Carter V Means the South's Not Dead, Either..............21

I Was Hoping That Character Wouldn't Get Killed Off. But I Understand.

Oscar Grant's America...35

The New Transported Man..41

824 Words..61

It Doesn't Feel Like Tupac's Been Dead
for 25 Years Because Sometimes It Doesn't
Feel Like Tupac Is Dead..65

Yeah, Let's Watch It Together. I'll Wait for You.

I Keep Saying I'm Never Coming Back
to Kanye But I Keep Coming Back
to His Verse on "Put On"..75

Inside of You, There Are Two Members of
the 1993 New York Knicks. One Knick Is
John Starks. One Knick Is Charles Smith........................77

I Don't Know What To Do About My Obama Shirt..........87

When CM Punk Changes His Theme
Music, You Must Change Your Life..................................93

When You Choose *Thor: The Dark World*
Over *12 Years a Slave*...99

On the Anniversary of Your Grandmother's
Death, You Remember...103

Scoot Back. You're Hurting Your Eyes.

My Dad Still Watches the NFL

This is about the old lion vs. the young lion. This is about the moderate and the progressive. This is about the father who's the same age as the four girls who got blown up in Birmingham and the son who married a white woman in Montgomery without the city bothering to blink. This is about the soldier and chef who raised the poet.

But it's not about that.

This is about a job. This is about how hard it is for some of us to get a job. This is about all the times we were told anyone would be lucky to have us on their team but we weren't a good fit for this team. This is about how it feels like we all got a good job when one of us gets a good job. This is about how much we love it when one of us says fuck this job and walks away. This is about how much we hate it when one of us says fuck this job and walks away because we know the next job might not ever become the next job. This is about how much we hate it when one of us says fuck this job and walks away because it reminds the world that we're not brave enough to say fuck this job and walk away.

But it's not about that.

This is about a quarterback kneeling. This is about how a quarterback kneeling can be the most beautiful or the most disappointing play in sports depending on the score. This is about all the times I called someone a bitch or a fag or a coward when they kneeled at the end of a *Madden* game instead of giving me another chance to hit them. This is about bravery and cowardice. This is about how you can only understand a quarterback kneeling if you understand the rules of the game. This is about game plans. This is about field position and risk. This is about offense and defense. This is about who has to worry about winning the game the right way and who just gets to worry about winning.

But it's not about that.

This is about my nonnegotiable loyalty to black quarterbacks. This is about what Randall Cunningham could have been with more talent on the outside. This is about Doug Williams answering that question at the Super Bowl. This is about never seeming to forget what Michael Vick did and never seeming to remember what Ben Roethlisberger did. This is about Tommie Frazier dragging the whole state of Florida behind him in the Fiesta Bowl. This is about Shaun King and second chances. This is about all the slot receivers and punt returners who could've been more. This is about everything y'all said about Jalen Hurts. This is about James Andrews owing a knee to RGIII. This is about seeing Cam Newton as a black quarterback before seeing Cam Newton as Auburn's quarterback. This is about how some of us get to be gunslingers and some of us get to be reckless. This is about how Tom Brady's MAGA hat was never an issue. This is about reading the field. This is about IQ. This is about leading the team.

But it's not about that.

This is about supporting our own. This is about leaving an extra dollar on the tip if the server is black. This is about seeing *Black Panther* opening night. This is about staying a little longer to talk to the only other student who looks like us. This is about paying extra for something we could have ordered off Amazon. This is about reminding anyone who will listen that there's a black-owned restaurant down the street, that there's a black-owned bank down the street. This is about how we decide who to cheer for in reality show competitions or government elections.

But it's not about that.

This is about labor and management. This is about who deserves to work and who deserves to toil. This is about black bodies and freedom and the terror that comes from putting the ideas of "black bodies" and "freedom" too close to one another.

But it's not about that.

This is about November 8, 2016. This is about how you were able to go to work the next day when your friends couldn't. This is about all the posts telling you the bad days were about to come when your skin and your name are the only timelines you need to know the bad days have been coming for a long time because the bad days were already here.

But it's not about that.

This is about the loneliness that comes with being a black man. This is about being lumped in with every other black man or being asked to step over every other black man. This is about the battle royale that leaves us all bloodied and blind. This is about wanting to be left alone but not trusting ourselves to be alone. This is about feeling like Jesus only because we know we're surrounded by Peters and Judases. This is about wanting to reach out but being afraid that the world will just see us as a black man reaching for something.

But it's not about that.

This is about staying up late with my brother and watching *Sportscenter* in the den while we waited for dad to come home with a box of chicken fingers from his second job as a hotel chef. This is about telling my dad who hit a homerun or who got traded after he falls into the recliner. This is about telling him who won the game and how while he dozes off to our postgame analysis. This is about the tradition of a father and son. This is about talking about the car transmission or apartment security deposit while we talk about Westbrook and LeBron on Christmas Day. This is about talking about the new job while we talk about if the Cowboys will ever fire Jason Garrett and if we can remember what happened to the most recently fired black coach.

But it's not about that.

This is about coming home for the first time since my parents retired. This is about my father sitting in the den recliner and watching the Cowboys with his great-granddaughter in his lap and smiling at her with a smile he only saves for the smallest of us. This is about my father saying his great-granddaughter pays more attention to the television when Alabama is playing because her four-month-old eyes know real football when they see it. This is about his great-granddaughter's eyes still being big enough to see the world as a question instead of seeing the world as a world of tired answers. This is about my father not having to ask what time it is so he can get ready to pick up a pan of chicken from the back fence of the hotel kitchen. This is about time and knowing there will always be a time for questions. This is about time and knowing there will always be a time for fighting. This is about time and knowing there will never be enough down time in the recliner to reclaim all the time stolen from my father and his father and his father and his father. This is about knowing that there's a time to fight and a time to sit down and love your father. This is about life and letting a black man live.

We Hate *Wonder Woman 1984* Because Nobody Ever Granted Our Wish

And we didn't wish for much. Not for a messiah who'd put their arm next to ours and raise their eyebrows when the world noticed we had the same skin tone. Not for fists strong enough to break a titan or feet that could carry us to the constellations. Not to settle the scores of our ancestors. We didn't dream of asking for a way home or a way to catch all of our names that were lost to the wind and ocean and earth. We didn't wish to catch lightning in our hand like a lazy foul ball or to hop out of an Escalade at our high school reunion wearing the armor of a god. We didn't even ask for a mind that could win over the brainy co-worker or win us enough money on *Jeopardy!* to buy our way out of the labyrinth of student debt portals. We just wished that the manager would call back when they said, "We'll keep in touch." We just wished that the bright brown eyes we fell in love with would call back when they said, "We'll keep in touch." We just wished the retirements would lead to an opening. We just wished the mirror wouldn't be so mean in the morning. We just wished for the power to resist the temptation of the first politician to visit our neighborhood and the first pretty face who asked us about our plans for the weekend. Somebody promised things would get better. Somebody promised dawn was coming after all this darkness. Somebody promised the world didn't care about accents. Somebody promised everybody was invited to this party. Somebody promised some day soon there would be someone looking for someone just like us. Somebody promised we could learn from Job as long as we didn't pay attention to the gods picking at the boils. Somebody promised that if we stayed on our knees long enough something godly would happen. But have you heard of the things that gods can do? Have you heard that the god who parted the seas is also the god who murdered the babies, that the god who sent his son to rid the world of monsters is also the god who turned his lover to ash when she begged to look him in the eye? And what is a wish other than a submission to something you can't see? Every wish is a prayer and every prayer is a submission to some god who might not have time for you, some god who might have more fun seeing just how many times they can own your tongue before they bother to let you know that they think this is really something you should handle on your own.

Watching Tennis Is the Whitest Thing I'll Ever Be Allowed To Do

I'm not as smart as people give me credit for. I've never completed a Rubik's Cube, *New York Times* crossword, or *Super Mario* game. Some people assume I'm smarter than I am because I'm a college teacher. I'm sure other people imagine me with more intellect than I actually have as a way to overcompensate for the other things they imagined about black men at one time or another. Celebrating my intelligence becomes a balance for the times they've voted to form a breakaway school district or shared the fake Bill Cosby "I'm Tired" rant. But this type of celebration carries its own burden. This type of celebration is a close relative of the celebrations we see when the audience claps after watching a dog shake hands or watching an elephant paint.

That's why I love watching tennis. No one expects me to know about tennis.

And I don't know much about it other than the basics. I know women have to win two sets while men have to win three. I know some players charge the net while others hug the baseline. I know Nadal is nearly unbeatable on clay, but I don't know why some players excel on certain surfaces. I know there are forehands and backhands, but I don't know when a player should use a forehand or backhand, and I love that I don't know any of these things when I let myself settle into the rhythm of the ball hitting the racquets and court, the rhythm of shoes shuffling and squeaking.

Like many of my life decisions, my choice to pay attention to tennis is related to my choice to root against my older brother. If he cheered for Andre Agassi, then I wanted to see Pete Sampras beat Andre Agassi. But my interest moved beyond a petty sibling rivalry when Monica Seles was attacked and stabbed on the court in 1993. If people were willing to stab other people over tennis, then the sport became more interesting to me. I couldn't understand the strategies and scoring system. But I could understand a rivalry. Seeing someone care so much made me care enough to watch when I remembered to watch.

But I grew out of the morbid curiosity and mostly grew out of the sibling rivalry. And that's what makes my love of tennis unique. It's a casual love. I normally dissect what I love. If you ask me about my love of history, I'll tell you about reading an Asimov book on the Dark Ages when I was in elementary school. And I'll mention that the Dark Ages are usually listed as lasting from 476 CE to 1099 CE. And I'll mention that the Battle of Hastings in 1066 CE is also an acceptable date for the end of the Dark Ages. And I'll mention that using 476 CE as the starting date is common, but the sack of Rome by the Ostrogoths in 476 CE wasn't much different than the sack of Rome by the Vandals in 455

CE and the sack of Rome by the Visigoths in 410 CE. If you ask me about my love of poetry, I'll take you back to me reading Homer's *Iliad* in elementary school and knowing I would spend the rest of my life telling the world Hector got jobbed. I don't love things that I can put away and ignore. But the impulse to dig deeper never touches me when I find a tennis match to watch during a lazy summer afternoon or during a night when I need background noise to keep me company while I'm grading. I'll raise my eyebrows at an upset. I'll try to remember if a player is the same player I watched last year. But I won't feel the urge to reach for my phone and search for a confirmation. I don't need a confirmation. I don't need to know anything more than who hit the ball and who missed.

If I passed Ashleigh Barty in the aisle at Publix, I wouldn't walk away thinking about sharing space with someone who retired as the best female tennis player on the planet. I'd walk away trying to figure out if her accent was Australian or English or South African. If my wife and I sat next to Stefano Tsitsipas at a restaurant, I wouldn't spend the meal sweating and sneering at him because my wife has a crush on him, and that's because I wouldn't know it was him. And besides, I wouldn't have to worry about Tsitsipas taking my wife because I imagine that, if he had the chance, he would open strong and fold when it was time to close just like he does in the majors.

When Serena Williams announced the 2022 US Open would be her last tournament, I watched and hoped she could find a way to win another major. But her eventual loss didn't sting anything like the sting I felt when Wilder lost to Fury for the first time or when Aldo ran into that left hand from McGregor. When Serena Williams lost, it didn't mean it was time for me to mourn and chew over how much she had to overcome to end up Crip Walking at Wimbledon. When she lost, it meant I could shrug my shoulders and go to bed.

There's a comfort in this ignorance that helps me understand the comfort that comes with other forms of ignorance. A life ignorant of the hounding eyes in a department store. A life ignorant of judgment carried by pens moving across notepads in interview rooms. A life ignorant of the doom that can come from police lights cutting through the calm of a rearview mirror.

I hate that I love the feeling, but I do love the feeling.

Tha Carter V Means the South's Not Dead, Either

On May 6, 2019, Lil Wayne announced he was going on tour with Blink-182, and the internet joked about it. The internet wanted to know if it was 2019 or 2009. The internet wanted to know who cared about Blink-182 or Lil Wayne. The internet wanted to know the last Blink-182 or Lil Wayne song that mattered.

I was happy the internet was making fun of the proposed tour because if the internet was making fun of a Lil Wayne tour that meant Lil Wayne was still alive to go on tour.

For the last few years, every time I saw Lil Wayne's name trending on Twitter or on a news ticker, I was sure he was dead. I would click his name or wait for the story after the commercial break. I was prepared to curse, argue with the nearest person about how Lil Wayne never got the respect that he deserved as a Southern artist. Even if the nearest person agreed with me, I'd still argue to make sure I said the words out loud.

I've been ready since the first reports of his seizures and overdoses surfaced in 2012. I was ready for Lil Wayne to die because I'm a professional wrestling fan, and professional wrestling might be the one genre of pop culture that can top hip-hop's list of artists who've died too young. Chris Benoit prepared me for Lil Wayne. Davey Boy Smith prepared me for Lil Wayne. Seeing Mick Foley find out about the death of one of his friends while Foley was doing a book signing in Tuscaloosa prepared me for Lil Wayne.

Lil Wayne going on tour was a sign of life. But, especially in the South, a sign of life doesn't mean the same thing as being alive.

Death doesn't know a middle ground in the South. Death is either a lightning bolt or a stream of syrup oozing to the edge of a plate. When my maternal grandmother died, there was an overheard conversation about a checkup and then a date for the funeral. I never knew my grandmother as sick or sickly. I knew her as my grandmother; she teased me about being too old to hug her. Then I knew my grandmother as dead. No pep talks to put on a happy face before we walked into the hospital room. I don't remember any prayer requests at the church that was two houses down from her old house. She was here with me, and then she wasn't.

Of course, that's not true. My maternal grandmother suffered from kidney problems for decades. She died at fifty-seven, and she spent almost half of those years dealing with kidney issues. But I didn't see that. I never knew her as my grandmother with kidney problems. I only learned about her kidney problems from reading her obituary twenty years later. I never knew her as dying. I only knew her as alive and then dead.

It happened the same way with friends from high

school. It happened the same way with my brother's father-in-law. It happened the same way with Rosewood, Florida. Things are here and then they are not. People are here and then they are not.

When the news and rumors of Lil Wayne's overdoses and seizures popped up in 2012, I figured his death would be another sudden Southern death, the kind that's really not sudden at all. We all knew about the Styrofoam cup. We all know what this country takes out of the South.

He didn't die, but he did decay. He went from rapping memorable punchlines to becoming a punchline. His rhymes became sloppy and predictable. The shocking stories about seizures and overdoses became just another story about seizures and overdoses.

Lil Wayne began to fade into the slow form of Southern death. Lil Wayne became the car parked in the yard for a small repair, the car that only needed a tune-up, the car that would get fixed once the summer job money came in. After a certain number of excuses, everyone knows the car will only leave the yard attached to a tow truck, but we still humor the dreamers who tell us the car is going to be back on the road again soon.

Lil Wayne became the cool mall that becomes the black mall that becomes the dangerous mall that becomes the abandoned mall. Lil Wayne became the bank that becomes a check cashing store. Lil Wayne became the Kmart that becomes an abandoned Kmart that becomes a discount clothing store that becomes an abandoned discount clothing store. Lil Wayne became the stores we only know by the names they had during our childhood even though people remind us of the new names every time we go home.

This slow form of death brings its own hope and hopelessness. This slow form of death reminds me of my paternal grandparents. They both suffered strokes a few years ago. My paternal grandfather, the only grandfather I've known, is also a diabetic. My grandfather was a journeyman/hustler who became a pastor. He loved to travel, but diabetes took one of his legs and his children took the car keys. He loves to tell stories, but there are times when the words just won't connect into a narrative. In a lot of ways, I learned storytelling and narrative from him because I watched professional wrestling with him. It was his knowledge of wrestling, not his knowledge of religion, that made his words unquestionable. And that made it even harder to watch him struggle with his words.

And it was hard to watch him struggle with his wife when I was able to visit them during the holidays or when I was back in Montgomery for the summer. My paternal grandmother has a sense of humor built on simple facts and observations. At their fiftieth anniversary celebration, she told the story of how her marriage almost didn't happen because she told my grandfather that she didn't date light-skinned boys. When I visited her in the hospital a few weeks after my own marriage in the summer of 2015, she told me not to worry about my courthouse marriage because people who have fancy weddings break up just like everybody else. They only have more bills to show for it.

Over the years following their strokes, talking with my grandparents became more valuable and more hurtful. My first ever family reunion was the lowest point. There were over a hundred of us in a large banquet hall in Montgomery. My family was bought and sold in Montgomery, and now we were gathered in Montgomery as survivors. As engineers, teachers, preachers, doctors. It should have felt like a celebration. My nieces and nephew danced together. I remembered to take a picture of my parents so I could have one more picture of them enjoying their recent retirements. I learned my father had an older brother who died as a child. I learned my great-great-great-great-grandfather was a slave owner and might have been one of the richest men in Montgomery. But all of this was overshadowed by the dread I felt when I saw my grandparents that night. I couldn't tell if they recognized me. They looked confused and overwhelmed by the noises and energy in the banquet hall. This could have been the last time I saw them alive. That night hurt. A part of me felt bitter. They lived long enough to make it to this family reunion, but they weren't alive enough to enjoy it.

My family history starts with my grandparents, and that means my family history starts in the South. And it's my allegiance to the South that makes me care about Southern artists like Lil Wayne. Lil Wayne was never my favorite rapper. I never had an overwhelming love for one of his songs or his lyrics. I've never listened to one of his albums with the same attention and intensity that I have when I listen to The Notorious B.I.G.'s *Life After Death* or OutKast's *ATLiens* or Big K.R.I.T.'s *Cadillactica*. Even during his best run, from 2003-2008, when many people were willing to agree with Lil Wayne's claim of being the best rapper alive, I was more interested in seeing if an artist like Cassidy would ever become more than a punchline battle rapper or if Juelz Santana's raps would ever move him beyond his status as the class clown of The Diplomats. Even amongst Southern rappers, I had more interest in T.I. and the persona he was working to create as King of the South.

By now, it's beyond boring to mention the connections we make with the art and artists that are part of our youth. We know the biases in place when we claim that our generation made the most memorable music or movies or cultural movements. I was born in 1984, so my adolescence was filled with the rise of Cash Money Records. I remember rolling my eyes when one of the guys from the neighborhood swore he recognized one of the girls in the "Back That Azz Up" video. I'm a fan of every "Cash Money Taking Over for the 99 and 2000" meme. Lil Wayne was part of that early Cash Money Records ensemble, but he was only a part of it. He didn't really establish himself as a solo act until the label started to fall apart in the early 2000s. By default, he became the star of the label when most of the other artists from the late 90s golden age left. "Back That Azz Up" wasn't his song. "Bling Bling" wasn't his song. Even with his talent, he became the focus of Cash Money Records simply because there wasn't anyone else to focus on. And he could've faded into hip-hop history like most of his other labelmates. He could've become a legacy act at the age of twenty-one. He could've been a featured artist on any of the "I Love the 90s" or "Throwback Hip-Hop" tours that have popped up recently. He could've been another artist that died with his label.

Instead, he turned himself into the best rapper alive.

Bravado is nothing new in hip-hop, but Lil Wayne's claim felt new for me because it was the first time I saw a Southern rapper make a claim that big without a modifier and make that claim stick. UGK were the Underground Kingz. T.I. was the King of the South. Even in a genre that begs artists to be as big and proud as possible, there was still a modifier attached to the South. There was still the stigma attached to the South even though Southern hip-hop has been the center of hip-hop for two decades.

The South is second place in America. To be Southern is to be *less than*. When I tell people I'm from Montgomery, Alabama, some people congratulate me on not having a strong accent. When I tell people I'm from Montgomery, Alabama, people give me stories about their grandparents and great-grandparents who made it out of Alabama. When I went to grad school in Miami, more than a few people congratulated me on making it out of Montgomery. I've listened to patronizing conversations about Soul Food and health because someone wanted to teach me about how the South eats its feelings.

When Lil Wayne was calling himself the best rapper alive, I was working on figuring out what to call myself. I was starting to come to terms with the idea that I was going to end up being a writer for the rest of my life, and being a writer meant that I thought I could do something special with the same twenty-six letters every other English speaker had at their disposal. As I finished undergrad and moved into graduate school, I had more and more opportunities to introduce myself and introduce my work. I almost soured on graduate school in Miami in the first month after a good night turned into a bad night at a restaurant next to my studio apartment. It was College Night, and a group of guys invited me to freestyle with them in the parking lot because they thought poets had to be rappers, too. I was probably more disappointed than they were when I had to tell them that I couldn't rap, but I nodded my head while I listened to drunk parking lot raps that sounded like drunk parking lot raps. I only remember the night because the last guy who rapped pulled me aside when we were all about to go back into the restaurant. He told me not to worry about the times the nonblack rappers said "nigger" while they were rapping. He said it was all love because "nigger" in Miami doesn't mean the same thing as "nigger" in Alabama.

When you're from the South, people assume you are dumb. People assume you don't know every definition of "nigger."

The same energy carried through workshop sessions where I had to listen to what it meant when a poet from Alabama talked about shackles in a poem. It followed me into happy hour socials where so many people told me how happy I was to be in Miami and out of the South.

I always loved home, but after grad school I realized that nothing I did was going to be separated from Montgomery, Alabama. I realized I didn't want to be separated from Montgomery, Alabama. If I was the best reader at an event, then the best reader came from Montgomery, Alabama. If I won a book prize, then Montgomery, Alabama, won a book prize. If Montgomery, Alabama, won a book prize, then my parents and grandparents and my whole family won a book prize.

When people learn that I'm from Montgomery, Alabama, I become something exceptional because I am something that's alive. The popular view of the South is the view of the South as dead, a black and white photograph. I admit, death has a special home in the South. The sudden deaths of Emmett Till, Addie Mae Collins, Carol Denise McNair, Cynthia Wesley, Carole Rosamond Robertson. The slow death of school integration. The slow death of voting rights. The slow death of diabetic rot. But I'm not the exception. The South is alive and defiant.

"Defiant" was one of the first words that came to mind when I found out Lil Wayne was finally going to release *Tha Carter V* in September 2018. He fought for years with his label and management to release the album. While he was fighting to release the album, the music that he did release didn't give me much room to be excited. His delivery felt labored. It felt like he was invited to be a guest on so many songs as a favor or matter of respect. At worst, it felt like pity for what Lil Wayne had become after nearly a decade of legal and health problems.

I was happy to hear that Lil Wayne finally came to a settlement with Cash Money Records and was going to release a new album, but I didn't plan on listening to the album.

In fact, insomnia pushed me to the album. I was up late writing about what I learned from my family reunion. I was writing to grapple with what it meant to discover the name of one of the men who owned and raped my ancestor. I'm sure part of me wanted to be angry when I put on my headphones and clicked on the album. I wanted another reason to be mad about what this country did and does to Southern black people. I was ready to mourn Lil Wayne. The music wouldn't let me do that.

Tha Carter V isn't a great album because Lil Wayne isn't a great rapper anymore, but I could hear some of the Lil Wayne I grew up with. He sounded like a rapper who would've called himself the best rapper alive, but he also sounded like a rapper who knew that "alive" was the most important word in the title. In his most joyful song, "Let It All Work Out," Lil Wayne admits—amongst a collection of inspirational clichés about perseverance and trusting fate—that he tried to commit suicide as a child and is thankful to be alive today. In "Let It All Work Out," the first words from Lil Wayne are a declaration: "I'm in this bitch." He repeats a version of this many times in the song. It's not a statement of bravado or dominance. It's a statement of defiance. It's a reminder to everyone, including Lil Wayne himself, that he's still here.

At the end of 2019, my wife and I visited my grandparents at their home when we were in Montgomery for Christmas. When we arrived, we were worried because they were home alone. We were ready to call around and make sure help was on the way, and after talking to my grandparents at the family reunion, I was ready for another difficult meeting that would sit on my soul for weeks, maybe longer.

But my grandparents assured us we didn't need to call anybody. My grandfather pulled me aside and told me stories about how men from his past came looking for him to settle an old score after he became a pastor. I could see the memory in his face. The men told him they didn't come to talk to Pastor McCall. They came to talk to Dan. And I smiled nervously, and happily, while he told me about the Creole women he remembered from his days in New Orleans. Later, I went into the other room and listened to my grandmother ask me about teaching. Then she told me and my wife about how she used to love to sing in the church choirs when she was younger. She complained about not being able to cook like she wanted to. She saw me and knew me. My grandfather saw me and knew me. I saw them and knew them again.

We are all dying. I'm closer to death now than I was three thousand words ago, but we don't all get to grow old. In Alabama, people complain that there's only two seasons: summer and not summer. A time of growth and heat, then a time of death. But like most weather complaints, the complaint isn't true.

There's a beauty to the fall in Alabama. Maybe I am partial to that beauty because I was born in October. We all know what it means when we have to put on long sleeves for the first time in months. We all know what it means to see our breath when we walk out of the door to meet the morning. We know the leaves will turn and fall, but there's a unique beauty to the yellowing leaves in the South. The leaves, stubborn, show off every color before they let go and descend. And there's a beauty in watching a rapper grow old because that means he's lived long enough to grow old. And there's a beauty in watching your grandparents wave death away to tell you one more story.

I Was Hoping That Character Wouldn't Get Killed Off. But I Understand.

Oscar Grant's America

I often joke about being "racially obligated" to do certain things. Cheer for the team with a black quarterback. Pretend the black politician doesn't lie like the other politicians. My friends laugh, and I laugh with them, but only part of me is joking. And that sense of obligation is what made me go see *Fruitvale Station*.

I knew the basics of the story, and if I didn't, the film started with the infamous cell phone footage of Oscar Grant being shot in the back by a cop. I knew it was coming, but I still gasped, and I still spent the next ninety minutes trying to find my breath.

For ninety minutes, I watched Michael B. Jordan portray Oscar Grant, a man under water. He's a man hoping for one more chance to make things right with his girlfriend, his job, his daughter, his mom. *Fruitvale Station* only shows us one day in his life, but that day explains the black male experience as well as the last twenty-five years of Spike Lee, the Hughes brothers, and John Singleton.

But *Fruitvale Station* is more than just the story of a black man with bad luck. It's a story about the foundation of the United States of America, and this country was founded on equal parts endurance and lies.

Fruitvale Station is a study in endurance, and endurance is an American virtue. We mythologized the Pilgrims' first winters, get as close as we can to praising the Confederate soldiers for holding the Union hordes back for so long. However, endurance is more than a virtue in the black community. Endurance. Grind. Hustle. They're just different names for the god worshipped in "We Shall Overcome," Sam Cooke's "A Change Is Gonna Come," and Tupac's "Changes."

Chance is another thread that travels through *Fruitvale Station*. Chance encounters show Oscar Grant's humanity and sense of humor. Chance encounters show his wavering fidelity and masculinity. Chance encounters lead to his death. In America, we love the idea of chance; we call our country a country of second chances. Really, it's a euphemism. America is a country of second chances because America is a country of lies. Our heroes—Jay Gatsby, John Smith, Marilyn Monroe—build their legacies on their lies and the depths they are willing to dare to turn those lies into reality. In America, we can look in the mirror one day and say, "That's not me." And if we try hard enough, the world might believe us. In America, we can make history out of whole cloth. We can change our fate. And throughout *Fruitvale Station*, I watched a man my age desperate to change his. Again, I knew how the story would end, but that didn't stop me from rooting for Oscar Grant when he promised he wouldn't get in trouble with the police again. That didn't stop me from shaking my head when the doctors gave the news to his family.

I'm not Oscar Grant; I'm an English teacher. However, Oscar Grant in *Fruitvale Station* is the current state of America. This is most evident when Oscar helps a pregnant woman find a bathroom and has a conversation with her husband. The husband admits his marriage didn't start smoothly. He admits he stole to put a ring on his wife's finger. His successful family was built on a lie. However, he forged that lie into his American dream. He starts as a thief, and he ends with a family and business cards to hand out to young black men looking to turn things around.

I know that guy. I went to school with that guy, lots of them. They bragged about not slowing down when they drove through a speed trap. After all, what can a cop do other than write a ticket? They knew they could get a Youthful Offender deal if the cop did manage to find the Ziploc bag under the driver's seat. They quit their jobs on gameday weekends because a job was just a job. Growing up (and even now, sometimes), that's what I wanted. Isn't that a certain type of equality? Doesn't being equal mean that I can give as few fucks as anyone else? But every time blue and red lights showed up in my rearview, I put two hands on the wheel and moved into the right lane.

In 2009, for me, and for African Americans in general, it felt like our years of diligence were finally being rewarded. We were getting a black president. I was getting a master's degree. The "American" in "African American" was the word that was starting to carry as much weight as the "African" in "African American." We made it to the White House. That had to count for something. I was a first-generation college kid who was on his way to making it. I could have been the poster child for what could happen when black boys pulled up their pants and opened a book. I wasn't the black boogeyman that made America reach for its guns. I wasn't going to have to explain to people that I went to college on an academic scholarship, not an athletic one. As a race, we could finally exhale. That's the lie so many of us were whispering to ourselves heading into 2009.

The murder of Oscar Grant should have shattered that lie, and it shouldn't have taken a movie, albeit a powerful movie, to cement his name as part of national conversations about race, violence, and justice. In many ways, Oscar Grant's death is tragic because it is so mundane in this country. A black man was shot to death. A black man was a victim of police violence. The black community calls for justice. Justice doesn't answer the call.

On the surface, there's nothing new here. But the police killed Oscar Grant on New Year's Day. He was killed on New Year's. *Fruitvale Station* keeps reminding viewers of that. New Year's is supposed to give everyone a clean record. For one day, we can forgive our friends' unrealistic dreams. For one day, we can kiss someone just because we're alive. We don't complain about the fireworks and gunshots and open beer containers. We celebrate this day because of its promise. This year could be the year. The year we find love. The year we finally get a good job. But New Year's Day is also another lie we've fallen in love with. At a New Year's party, I'm the lame guy who will slap people on their shoulders and ask them about their goals for the next year. I make goals. Years ago on New Year's Day, I looked in the mirror and promised myself I would get a book deal. It was a dumb promise, but my first book contract came in the mail a few months later. I know it's really just a date on a calendar, but I believe anyway.

But it's just a date on a calendar. We love the myth of America because we love the idea of being able to leave our past behind. But, more often than not, the world won't let us forget who we are. Months and years can fall off the calendar like dead leaves. January 1 starts a new year, but it doesn't make the bills on the counter disappear. The scars don't melt away when the ball drops in Times Square. In *Fruitvale Station*, Oscar Grant does his best to make a new way for himself. But he can't. His identity dooms him. Someone calls his name, and that leads to a bullet in his back.

During the last few moments of the film, I heard a few sniffles in the theater. We weren't crying because it was a surprise. No matter how much I wanted to yell at the screen when Oscar decides to take the train home, I knew it was going to happen. No matter how much I wanted the doctors to give good news to his family, I knew it wasn't going to happen. We knew how this story was going to end; that's where the pain came from. We know that it doesn't matter who sits in the White House. It doesn't matter how much blood was spilled in Alabama. It doesn't matter how many laws are protected or gutted by the Supreme Court. Being black in America is still being black in America. 2009 changed a lot of things, but it didn't change the color of our skin.

When I left the theater, two younger guys were in front of me. Baggy shorts, big T-shirts. They could have been cover models for a Bill O'Reilly op-ed on wild black boys. But there was no wildness in their eyes. There was no swagger in their walk as we left the dark theater and stepped into the light of a Friday afternoon. I thanked them for holding the door for me. I'm pretty sure my voice cracked, and I'm pretty sure they noticed. They didn't laugh. They didn't smirk at the grown man who got shook up by a movie. For a few seconds, the three of us allowed each other to escape expectations. After *Fruitvale Station* gave us a sobering dose of reality, the three of us took advantage of the chance to live in a lie, no matter how small it was.

The New Transported Man

Honest people make the best liars.
I am a very honest person.
I am a very good liar.

I. The historian writes dates on a timeline and declares that these exact things happened on these exact dates. The historian is honest, but history is a liar.

I can remember dates. I can impress my wife by recalling the day we met. I can win points in a happy hour debate by dropping the date of a battle or movie release into my conversation with any group of tipsy intellectuals. I can list all the dates that led me to think about myself as a writer and to think about how the world made me a writer.

The day I was born.
The day my grandmother died.
The day I took my first creative writing class.
The day John Starks dunked on Michael Jordan.
The day Lil Wayne almost made it back to sounding like Lil Wayne.

The day my first book was published.

Honestly, the liar in me says all these days matter to me and all these days made me the writer I am today and the person I am today.

Honestly, only one day matters, and that's the day that a college kid died so that I could live.

This is where I want to say that I was that college kid, but this is where I still struggle with how to view suicide. My mind is divided on suicide in the same way some Christian denominations are divided on the idea of sin. Some denominations argue that sin begins with action. Lust starts at the first touch. Idolatry starts once the first animal is laid on the altar of the false god. Other denominations believe that sin begins when the mind moves towards the sin. Satan's first dream of rebellion becomes just as sinful as the first blood drawn in the war for heaven. Mankind's decline begins with the apple in Eve's mind, not Eve's mouth.

For me, the latter definition of sin feels truer, and the latter definition feels closer to how I view myself after I decided to kill myself on November 13, 2005.

November 13, 2005. That's the only day that matters and the only day that will ever matter for me. It's my second birthday, but that's not uncommon. Many people have a second birthday. It might be the day someone leaves their hometown in the rearview mirror. It might be the day someone finds religion. It might be the day someone walks out of prison. For me, it was the day I walked into a psych ward for the second time and figured out how to leave myself behind.

I came across a theory on suicidality recently, and the idea of suicidal thoughts as a condition detached from any mental illness or defect was a revelation. It's dangerous for me to say this, but thinking about what it would mean to kill myself is a regular thought for me. Admitting this puts my career in danger. Admitting this will hurt people I love and hurt people who gave so much of themselves to make sure I did not give my life away. But, remember, this essay is the honest essay. I drive and think about drifting into the median. I think about rivers and my inability to swim. I've spent entire plane rides thinking about the exit doors over the wings.

I can write the above paragraph with the full confidence that those thoughts won't affect my day any more than my thoughts of what it would be like to have Superman's x-ray vision or Professor X's telepathic powers. They're thoughts. Empty variables. Mind games inside of a mind that never figured out how to turn itself off.

Since November 13, 2005, my thoughts of suicide have been empty because I did kill myself. The fantasies are redundant.

A restlessness drives me. The restlessness makes writing attractive to me because I know I will never finish being a writer. Early in our relationship, my wife noticed that she celebrated my writing accomplishments much longer than I would celebrate them. There have been times when friends have congratulated me and I've needed a reminder of why they were congratulating me. This doesn't mean that accomplishments don't drive me. There's a certain egotism that drove me to write and still drives me to write. I have a map of Alabama literature and literary figures in my campus office. The map shows where prominent Alabama authors lived and has markers to show the location of books set in Alabama. Zelda Fitzgerald is the author listed next to Montgomery, Alabama. Montgomery is my hometown. A generation or three from now, when they make the next map of Alabama literature and literary figures, I want my name to replace Zelda Fitzgerald's name. But even if I went to my office tomorrow and saw my name on that map, I would still come back to my latest poem and grumble over whether the enjambments meet the standards for enjambments I was given by Leah Nielsen.

The restlessness makes teaching attractive because I know I will never finish learning how to be a teacher. Each class is its own lesson in failure. Even if most of my class evaluations are positive, I always leave a class, leave a semester, planning on how I can make a smoother connection between poetic form and poetic arguments or planning for how I can make a connection between the xenophobia in *Othello* and the xenophobia in *Medea*. I want to do better because I want to do better for my students. I often tell my students that once they walk into my classroom, they are part of my team, and I tell them that I love seeing my team win. But even if I didn't care about my responsibility to my students, I'd still lose hours considering edits to my syllabi and grading scales.

Today, my restlessness is a directed restlessness. A controlled burn.

In 2005, there was no direction or control. There was only restlessness and burning. In 2005, I was moving from my sophomore to junior year in college. My junior year of college was supposed to be the year the world began to bend to the will of a twenty-one-year-old man. I used to talk about the transition from lowerclassmen to upperclassmen a lot with my friend Danny. We went to high school together, and he was a year ahead of me. We spent more than a few nights drinking on his porch and philosophizing about how there was a certain turning point in a college guy's tenure on campus. We'd have most of these conversations on those nights when "just one more beer" turned into a night of many beers and many laughs and many silences that weren't awkward or pregnant. We laughed about the adolescent insecurities we brought to college with us. We laughed about the shit liquor and shittier beer we drank because it was the only thing to drink at the party. We laughed about the mouths we kissed because we needed to know there was someone in the world who wanted to kiss us even if the shit liquor and shittier beer were the only things that made them want to kiss us. We talked about figuring out majors and minors and figuring out what it meant to be weird art school kids from the first capital of the Confederacy who were figuring out life on the campus where George Wallace called for segregation forever. Those conversations felt like a turning point. Those conversations made me feel like I was growing because I wouldn't have been able to have those conversations a year earlier. The hard work of being a thinker, a dreamer, and a good guy was starting to pay off.

I remember these conversations because they were close to the truth for me, but they also couldn't have been farther from the truth for me. I was starting to get the things I wanted out of myself and out of life. I convinced my parents to let me study abroad in Greece in the Summer of 2005. In Greece, I ran a race in the original Olympic stadium. I carried my body that had been fueled by Natural Light, cheap gin, and Arby's for the last two years up Mount Olympus. My life was threatened in the backroom of a Greek dive bar. My study abroad cohort and I rapped The Notorious B.I.G.'s verse from "Mo Money Mo Problems" in the streets of Athens when the DJ in the bar changed the song after Diddy's verse. I had a passport and a dozen stories to tell my friends, family, and any pretty face I was brave enough to sit next to at a party once I made it back to Alabama. And some girls actually did come back to the couch when they left and said they were just going to get another drink. Bartenders didn't ask what I was having because they knew my name and had my favorite drink waiting for me a minute after the bouncer handed my ID back to me. The conversations with family and friends started to shift from "How are you liking college?" to "What's next after college?" because my family and friends had already decided I would conquer college. They had decided I would make it out and become something bigger than a kid from Montgomery with a good set of parents. I finally gave in to my love of ancient history and became a Classics major. I finally decided writing might not just be a hobby and decided to minor in Creative Writing.

I was always a good student in my creative writing classes. I could always dig up a mythology or history reference to earn my share of head nods and gasps in workshop, but I never really saw myself as someone who could be a *writer* until my junior year of college. I was in my first upper-level creative writing class. It was a poetry workshop. Everyone in the room was an English major, someone who wanted to go to graduate school for creative writing, or someone who had a comic book script they wanted to show me over the weekend. It was an exciting and supportive room. And I loved the room until I realized I was the best writer in the room.

When the conversations in the workshop started to transform into coronations for the two or three class favorites, I managed to smile through the praise, offer sincere feedback to my classmates (I didn't realize I was falling in love with the idea of helping other writers), and watch the clock until I could leave and meet my friends for the 2 p.m. to 11 p.m. happy hour at El Rincon, the Mexican restaurant next to campus.

And then I found myself watching the clock at El Rincon.

And then I found myself watching the clock in the mornings after I kissed a girl goodbye and told her we'd talk later about what we were doing for the weekend.

It was the opposite of a Midas Touch, the opposite of alchemy. Everything I wanted was in my grasp, and everything I touched slowly turned into lead.

There was a psych ward visit a week before November 13, 2005. I woke up on a Sunday morning and drove to the closest bridge I could find. It was an overpass, and I sat on the edge and watched cars pass by under me. There was no plan to jump. I didn't even think of myself as a man dangling himself on the edge of a bridge until I heard someone from a passing car yell, "Don't do it."

The police showed up, and I was in the hospital hours later.

The hospital conversations weren't much different than the classroom conversations. I was a promising young man. I just had to get control of my emotions. I was told that writers are sensitive people, and sensitive people have these outbursts.

I nodded my head. I joked. I promised I wouldn't be a letdown to all the patients and staff who wished me luck and promised me I had the whole world at my fingertips.

I walked out of the hospital after the seventy-two-hour hold was over. I went back home and went back to watching the clock.

November 13, 2005, was a Sunday, and there was an Alabama football game the day before. Alabama lost to LSU. It was our first loss of the season, an overtime heartbreaker that served as a reminder that our dream season was only a dream. But plans had already been made. There was a house party to attend. There was beer to drink and friends to meet up with so that we could joke and curse about the game. There were only a few more football weekends in the year, so, win or lose, I was supposed to make the most out of these last weekends of football and afterparties.

When I describe suicidality to people who can't imagine ever wanting to kill themselves, I describe it as the feeling of wanting to leave a party. It can be a boring party. It can be an exciting party. But most people know the feeling of reading the room, reading themselves, and knowing there's not a bone in their bodies that wants to be at the party one more second than they have to be there.

Of course, in this description, life is the party, and I've always felt a pull to leave this party behind.

But that comparison isn't completely abstract. It isn't abstract at all. I decided to kill myself at the house party that started the Saturday night after the Alabama vs. LSU game and moved into Sunday morning. I was talking to a girl I had never met before. We were laughing and had made it to the point in the conversation where one of us was supposed to ask if the other person was on Facebook yet. One of us was supposed to ask for a phone number. One of us was supposed to ask if the other one was hungry or needed a ride home. One of us wasn't supposed to walk away, walk out of the house, and start sending goodbye text messages to friends and family, but that's what I did.

II. The wrestler holds his fist up to the crowd and promises to punch his opponent in the face. The wrestler is honest, but wrestling is a lie.

Eddie Guerrero died on November 13, 2005. He was one of my favorite wrestlers. He was found like many wrestlers are found: lifeless in a hotel room. The cause of death was listed as a cardiac arrest, but living as a professional wrestler for twenty years killed Eddie Guerrero. He had been sober for a number of years and had enjoyed a run as WWE World Champion in 2004, but most of his career was filled with bouts of alcoholism, steroid use, and painkiller addictions. His heart gave out when he was thirty-eight. He was an example of a recovery story. He was a born-again Christian. Fans loved the persona he developed and how his performances echoed his most popular catchphrase of "I lie. I cheat. I steal." He rode a lowrider to the ring and made the wrestling world cheer or boo him depending on his mood. He could make the same people who chant "build the wall" today wear his T-shirt and slap their chests with pride. He could also make fans boo with all their might as he portrayed the Latino menace who had come to rob the United States of its moral compass and its championship belts.

That's what I liked most about Guerrero. I loved his ability to change himself. His family was a wrestling dynasty in Mexico and the Southwestern U.S., and he helped popularize the quick and high-flying Mexican Lucha Libre style of professional wrestling in the United States. But even though his name and family history would always point to the Mexican professional wrestling tradition, Guerrero could wrestle any style. He was an expert in Japanese strong style wrestling, which focuses on realistic strikes and submission holds. He was an expert in the United States style of wrestling that rewards theatrics and crowd interaction as much as it rewards athletic skill.

Many of the greatest stars in Mexico and Japan wear masks or face paint to give them a unique appearance or to help audiences know the wrestler's backstory. Early in his career, Guerrero wrestled in a mask as Black Tiger. But at his best, he didn't need a mask. He could wear any face that he wanted, and I loved him for that.

He was a master of persona. He could fake any emotion, but calling him fake is just as reductive as calling professional wrestling fake. His impact on the audience and his peers was beyond real, and I saw that impact when I watched wrestling the Monday night after I had been placed in the psych ward for the second time. I remember the male and female patients arguing over the television, and somehow professional wrestling was the compromise. The second I saw the black armbands the wrestlers were wearing, I knew someone had died.

The beauty of professional wrestling is also what makes professional wrestling grotesque. It's a funhouse mirror for the world, but sometimes the funhouse mirror shows a more honest version of the world than anyone wants to see. Ever since I was a graduate student, people have constantly recommended Roland Barthes' essay on wrestling to me once they learn I'm a professional wrestling fan. Barthes' analysis about how wrestling is built on archetypes and national fears and hopes is supposed to be insightful, but any wrestling fan who knows what the word "archetype" means could write the same essay. Sgt. Slaughter became an Iraqi sympathizer in 1991 so that Hulk Hogan could have a foreign menace to defeat at WrestleMania VII. Every wrestling villain knows the quickest way to rile up a crowd is to make a joke about the hometown sports team. Fans love the absurdity of professional wrestling because we are part of the absurdity. Fans love the absurdity of professional wrestling because there's a sense of control.

When real-world events break through the veil of professional wrestling, that control dissolves. In 1999, Owen Hart fell to his death during a wrestling event when his harness broke and an arena full of people watched him fall like Icarus. They stopped the event long enough to get him out of the arena and out of view, but they didn't cancel the show. Instead, the company chose to turn the next day's televised show into a memorial show. Storylines were abandoned for a day. Characters were allowed to speak as individuals. Owen Hart was celebrated as a person.

The night after Eddie Guerrero died, the company held a memorial show as well, and I remember watching and thinking about how these moments in professional wrestling reminded me of the funerals in Homeric poems. I thought of the Greeks pausing to mourn and celebrate Patroclus and then later pausing to mourn and celebrate Achilles. I thought of Priam and Achilles negotiating the terms for the mourning of Hector.

And like many heroes from world traditions, Eddie Guerrero was a victim of hubris. Being a great comedic performer wasn't good enough for him. Being a scrappy underdog wasn't good enough for him. Being a stereotypical foreigner with a mission to expose the wrongs of the United States wasn't good enough for him. I know Guerrero's heart gave out because of decades of substances and pain, but I've always had the idea in my head that Guerrero died from exhaustion. He simply pushed himself into death.

I like that version of Guerrero's death because it's attractive to imagine us dying on the same day and me meeting him in the line of souls waiting to move from this world to the next one. We would've talked about his favorite matches. I would've told him about how my grandfather taught me to love wrestling. Then we would've asked each other how we ended up dead, and we would have shared a bond of being two people who pushed themselves too hard and pushed themselves out of their bodies. That dream is better than the dream of meeting the Eddie Guerrero who died just as he was moving into the best and cleanest years of his life. The Eddie Guerrero who died just as he was moving into the best and cleanest years of his life might not have much time for a college kid who killed himself because he couldn't find any joy in house parties, occasional hookups, and poetry classes.

The psych ward facility was underground, and like people who travel to the underworld and back, I don't remember everything. I remember my anger and jealousy while I watched wrestling the day after Guerrero died. I remember Tuesday's lunch had an option for chicken fingers, but I was released before lunch. When I'm ranking my favorite chicken fingers, I sometimes wonder where the psych ward chicken fingers would've ranked on the list. I remember speeches from black staff members about how I needed to fix myself because the community needed good black men. I remember the speeches about how I just needed a good woman to take my mind off of killing myself.

But mostly, I remember my mother.

III. The mother promises the child that the pain will go away. The mother is honest, but pain is a liar.

My parents visited me in the hospital. We sat in therapy sessions and listened to the doctor assure me that I needed a good doctor when I left the hospital. He also assured me that I couldn't afford him as a doctor. As we went through the sessions each day, he complimented me on my improved posture and complimented me for moving from an "11" to a "3" on the 1-to-10 scale of how much I wanted to end my life. My family isn't the type of family that makes elaborate plans, or maybe I've been able to present a front that's made my family believe I never needed an elaborate plan. I was never a problem child. I got a bad conduct report in sixth grade. My mother caught me with beer in my car during my senior year. A couple of girls came over when I had the house to myself. But I went to gifted schools and had college scholarships waiting for me, so all was forgiven or ignored. When we talked about college, my parents only wanted to know how things were going and if I needed money or if I needed help moving from one apartment to the next. My parents love through support, and support is a monumental form of love. But, in hindsight, my parents probably should've insisted that I come home or at least take a semester off after my second time in the psych ward. They should've at least asked about the drinking because all of the other black people in the hospital seemed to be mad about my drinking.

But I suspect my parents know me and know my restlessness more than they've ever let on. And maybe that's why the only plan came from my mother. When they were about to leave the psych ward, she hugged me and said, "Don't leave me."

The more pleasant essay would say those words were an elixir, that those words brushed away all of the doubt and restlessness in my head. But this isn't the pleasant essay; this is the honest essay. My mother's words worked because I was able to trade one obsession for another. I promised my mother I wouldn't leave her, but that promise isn't a promise I only made once while I was in the psych ward. I make that promise every day when I wake up. I live up to that promise every time I don't let the dreams of drifting into the median become anything more than dreams.

Keeping a promise is a never-ending task. There have been over five thousand days since I gave that promise to my mother, and I've remade that same promise at the beginning of every day for over five thousand days. Doing something for five thousand days becomes its own habit, of course. But one habit doesn't always replace a previous habit. The thoughts of keeping my promise to my mother haven't removed the thoughts of suicide. And if the natural order of things prevails and my promise to my mother prevails, I will outlive my mother. And if I outlive my mother, I'll have to decide what to do with my promise to my mother.

Keeping my promise to my mother means that I return to November 13, 2005, every day. And every day, I bury the person who decided to kill himself on November 13, 2005. Returning to November 13, 2005, is, of course, just another restlessness. Just another need that's not far from the needs that pushed me out of my body that day. I can't count the number of *CSI* or *Law & Order: SVU* episodes I've watched where the heroes catch the killer because the killer can't resist coming back to the scene of the crime. I come back to November 13, 2005, in my writing. I come back to November 13, 2005, when a song from that period pops up in my playlists. But mostly, I come back to November 13, 2005, because there's always a body to bury from November 13, 2005.

IV. The magician shows his empty hands to the audience before announcing his next trick. The magician is honest, but magic is a lie.

Christopher Priest's 1995 novel *The Prestige* (which is the basis for the 2006 Christopher Nolan film of the same name) focuses on the feud between two magicians and how that feud controls the lives of the magicians and their families for generations. Alfred Borden is a purist. He takes great care to preserve the traditions of magic. He makes every effort to respect the core values of the discipline. He meets his rival, Rupert Angier, by discovering Angier is using magician's techniques to host staged seances for gullible and grieving audiences. Angier is obsessed with the results of magic: the money, the fame, the response from wowed audiences. The rivalry reaches its climax as both men compete to create the best version of the trick that Borden names "The Transported Man." In the trick, Borden appears to instantly move himself from the main stage to another part of the theater. The answer to the magic trick is obvious. If no one can be two places at once, then Borden must have a body double. But the simple answer is not a satisfying answer to Angier. The success of the trick maddens Angier, and he goes to every end to discover the secret behind his rival's greatest trick. His restlessness leads him to a fictionalized Nikola Tesla, who builds him a machine that will transport a man from one place to another.

Angier's restless and reckless pursuit of his rival leads to the creation of a cloning machine, and Angier clones himself on stage to the applauses of ever-growing audiences. He endures an immense pain every time he steps into the cloning device, but he eventually becomes addicted to the pain. He becomes addicted to the ability to remake himself at will. This addiction supersedes his rivalry, his avarice, and even his love for his family. But the cloning machine leaves behind an obvious problem. The machine leaves behind an extra body that must be dealt with.

My wife only tolerates the film version of *The Prestige* because David Bowie plays Tesla in the film. I've never told her why I like the film more than she does. I'm drawn to *The Prestige* because I know the allure of recreation. I watched the film before I discovered the novel. I don't have a special interest in magic, and, initially, I imagine I was attracted to the movie because of the aura of intellect that surrounded Christopher Nolan in the mid 2000s. But it wasn't the directing or the performances of Christian Bale, Hugh Jackman, or Scarlett Johansson that pulled me into the film. It was the restlessness at the heart of the story. There's an irresistible allure to transform the body into something more. And, really, transformation is at the heart of my thoughts of suicide. Most of those thoughts don't linger on judgment or an afterlife. Most of those thoughts linger on the chance to turn myself into something else.

There's an allure to the pain that comes with reshaping my face so the world doesn't see all the dead versions of me hiding behind my face. Hiding those bodies becomes harder as the body count grows, but the emotion behind hiding those bodies fades with each new corpse. Over five thousand days since November 13, 2005. Over five thousand bodies between the person who died on November 13, 2005, and the person writing these words.

This is the honest essay, and honestly, there is a magic to making the world see me as someone other than a man who decided to die in 2005 because I am someone other than a man who decided to die in 2005. I am a successful teacher and writer. There's a magic to having colleagues view me as a model of stability because I have been stable and healthy for years. There's a magic to making some students believe I can help them navigate college even though college killed me. My death in college is the primary reason I can help some students navigate college.

I sign my name as "Jason McCall." My records start in 1984 and carry on to today, but the signature is a lie. The dates on the passports and licenses are a lie. There's no way I can be the same person I was before I left that party and told the world goodbye. But there's no way I could be anything else, either. This is the trap that I struggle to escape from. This is the trap I love and long for. The laws of conservation say that nothing is ever really gained or lost. The laws of conservation say that the body that walked into the psych ward had to walk out of the psych ward because a body cannot be in two places at once. The only truth is that someone named Jason McCall walked into a psych ward on November 13, 2005, and someone named Jason McCall walked out of the same psych ward three days later. The only truth is that I am a very good liar who's getting better every day.

824 Words

I'm still learning how to be sad about Kobe because I'm still learning how to be sad about myself.

I'm sad that Kobe died because I'm still learning how to see peers as companions and not competition. I'm still learning that every trophy they raise isn't a trophy stolen from my case. I'm still learning that success doesn't have to come with a snarl and a flex. I'm still learning that compliments don't have to have a sublevel to them. I'm still learning that every smile isn't just about flashing my teeth. I'm still learning what it means to share space with this golden age of Southern writers and artists. I'm still learning that throwing up a link to an Ashley M. Jones poem or an Imani Perry essay is just as good as throwing it up to Shaq in Game 7 against the Blazers.

I'm sad that Kobe died because I'm still learning how to deal with the man I used to be. Maybe I wasn't a predator, but I was predatory, and I know there are women who hear my name as a curse that conjures up a hand, breath, or mouth that should have never been there. I'm still learning that everyone shouldn't forgive me. I'm still learning that everything I've done since my worst days doesn't change what was done on my worst days.

I'm sad that Kobe died because Kobe was corny. The Mamba Mentality wasn't anything that Hulk Hogan didn't tell me when he told me to train, say my prayers, and eat my vitamins. The Mamba Mentality wasn't anything that Goku didn't show me when he found another galactic sensei to help him reach a more final final form. The Mamba Mentality is corny, but it's genuine. The Mamba Mentality is about effort and craft, and black people don't get credit for effort and craft. Black success is either effortless grace or animal instinct. The idea of black greatness as a product of black effort and black craft is a dangerous idea because effort and craft are products of the mind and to acknowledge black effort and black craft is to acknowledge the black mind.

I'm sad that Kobe died because Kobe was teaching me that changing a uniform wasn't enough to change an identity. My work clothes might change. My budget for my work clothes might change. My shared office might become a single office. The title in front of my name might make people respect my name. But none of that erases where I started. None of that allows me to buy into the American myth of reinvention. To be black is to be layered like the levels of the planet. Mantle, crust, core all spinning and growing and withering together. I'm still looking for a plot to bury the dreams of the twenty-year-old I sacrificed on the altar to make sure the gods would favor the forty-year-old. I'm still trying to figure out how to be both Iphigenia with the knife at her neck and Agamemnon with the knife in his hand. I'm still trying to figure out how to slit my own throat and keep the blood off my new shirt.

I'm sad that Kobe died because my sports heroes shouldn't die before my dad's sports heroes. Kobe being dead while Michael Jordan is alive is another reason to grit my teeth at the Boomers and their refusal to get out of the way. I wanted to see Kobe have a chance to be a bad NBA coach, a bad general manager, a bad late night talk show host. Kobe had a chance to be in Hollywood and be a cheerleader for his daughters, but I wanted to see Kobe have a chance to do more. Kobe was a bad rapper, and I feel cheated because I won't see Kobe be bad at a billion more things. I wanted to see Kobe sell bad home gyms. I wanted to see Kobe sell bad Italian-Japanese fusion food. I wanted Kobe to have a billion bad ideas and I wanted to forgive him for being bad because he put up eighty-one points and he shot a free throw with a torn Achilles.

I'm sad that Kobe died because I don't want to learn from another dead black man. America wants me to learn from the bones of Malcolm and Martin and Ali and John Henry without discussing who turned Malcolm and Martin and Ali and John Henry into bones. America wants me to learn from dead black men so that I can remember that I, too, can be a dead black man in the next instant. If I'm lucky, I can be a lesson for the next group of black boys lucky enough to live in a country with an endless supply of dead black men to admire. I'm sad that Kobe died because I'm sad about another dead black man.

It Doesn't Feel Like Tupac's Been Dead for 25 Years Because Sometimes It Doesn't Feel Like Tupac Is Dead

Tupac died in 1996. And, as a son of Alabama and a son of the South, I'm supposed to remind everyone that while Tupac and B.I.G. were fighting over East Coast vs. West Coast supremacy, Big Boi and Andre let the world know that "The South got somethin' to say" at the 1995 Source Awards, and that declaration is a main reason why Southern hip-hop has led the way for hip-hop and American music ever since. But better writers can tell that story better than I can. That's a story better left in the hands of Kiese Laymon or Regina N. Bradley.

But when the radio told me Tupac died on September 13, 1996, I wasn't thinking about how his death was making room for Southern voices in hip-hop. I was thinking about how his death was taking away space for a black boy like me.

Tupac's death wasn't an opening. It was a void.

I hesitate to say "boy" because I was eleven when Tupac died, in that space when black boys morph into black males. Sadly, many black boys don't make it to eleven before they are met with the world of toil and torture our country reserves for black males, but I was lucky. My voice and shoulders were starting to take up more space. More realities reached my mind whenever a girl slapped my arm after I made a joke in the lunch line.

But once I moved into that space between black boy and black male, there was less room for jokes in the lunch line. There was less room for jokes and more orders from teachers to keep our mouths shut and to keep to one side of the hallway. There were more warnings about how we needed to get the foolishness out of our systems before we went to junior high.

Now, I know most of those teachers, mostly black women, weren't warning us about junior high. They were warning us about how the world was starting to see us. How the wrestling matches after school would look like brawls. How the art we created with our shoelaces to make ourselves feel better about the clearance rack Reeboks we wore would soon be seen as proof of gang affiliation. They were letting us know that we were dangerous no matter how many times we said we were just joking, just playfighting, just liked the way the red laces looked in the shoes.

Tupac's death, and the lack of justice that followed, was a concrete example of how the world could treat black men who looked like a threat, but even before he died, Tupac taught me that the world would see some of us as dangerous no matter what we did, no matter if we wore our pants on our hips or waist, no matter if we went to "Peter Crump the city dump" (the unfortunate nickname of my elementary school that stemmed from the gathering of garbage trucks in the school parking lot every Saturday) or if we went to the gifted school and sat next to the governor's daughter. But, despite the obvious risk, a lot of boys love seeing men act dangerous and fearless. I learned about fearlessness from watching Deion Sanders and Michael Irvin fight for position in the 1994 NFC Championship Game. I learned about the power of being dangerous and fearless from watching the way my older sisters would scramble for the remote when 2 Live Crew videos popped up on the TV in the den.

But seeing Tupac living dangerously, fearlessly, and free was different because I got to see so many different faces of Tupac. Even as a preteen, I knew that black boys were supposed to pick a primary lane, maybe dabble in a secondary lane here and there, and live in that primary lane for as long as they were allowed to live. There was respect for the athlete. There was respect for the artist. There was respect for the comic. And, despite the stereotypes that claim black communities don't value education, there was respect for the geek. That doesn't mean these lanes couldn't overlap. The comic could hoop. The geek might pull out a nice punchline in the bathroom rap battles, but there were lanes. There were expectations.

I was attracted to Tupac because Tupac had a song for everything. I knew black people were people, and that meant we held a universe of personhood inside of us. I saw that at home and in my neighborhood, but it meant something different to see it on TV and hear it on the radio. It meant something to know the same artist could make "Brenda's Got a Baby" and "Hail Mary" and make me believe he meant every word in each of them. There was—and still is—something special about believing in the thug talk even though we all knew he went to art school with Jada Pinkett Smith and we saw him dancing with Digital Underground. Even if we knew some of it was fake, it was all real. Seeing Tupac's imagination reinforced what I knew about all the possibilities available for black imagination and black personhood.

My relationship with Tupac and his ghost is naturally tied to my relationship with youth and possibility. One of my favorite hip-hop memories will always be walking home from school the week after "California Love" came out. Me and my friend Terry went back and forth rapping the song while walking down the sidewalk feeling like the hardest boys to ever walk down the sidewalks of Woodley Park. We didn't notice that there was no profanity in Tupac's verse. We felt like we were saying the most dangerous words on Earth when the first lines of "Out on bail, fresh out of jail" left our lips and rang through the neighborhood. For that one walk home, our neighborhood was transformed into a Mad Max hellscape, and we were the baddest duo to ever set foot on that sand. But even at that age, I knew I was playing out a fantasy that would likely never touch me. In this part of Montgomery, I knew the only people who might really see me as a thug were the police, and their opinions only counted if they decided to reach for the trigger or the cuffs. But even if I knew I could never have Tupac's flash, I had his words and energy. And when his words and energy came off as contradictory or inconsistent, it was a lesson that there was room for me to be contradictory or inconsistent as long as it felt real to me.

This isn't about Tupac as a role model or his deification. My grandfather, father, uncles, cousins, older brother, and teachers all showed me different examples of what it meant to be a "good black man," but all these examples also showed me how easy it could be to be labeled a "good black man" when so many people were hungry to find a "good black man." A black man who can tie a tie is held up as a good black man. A black man who keeps his eyes open in class is a good black man. When Tupac was convicted of first-degree sexual abuse, some people said it was proof that he was a good black man because the world always wants to lock up a good black man. Seeing Tupac get put in prison didn't make me question whether or not he committed a crime; it made me question what I could get away with, how much suffering I could bring into the world and have someone try to hide it under the shroud of me being a "good black man." Admitting that I love Tupac means that I have to admit that I love someone who went to prison for assaulting a woman, and my love of Tupac might mean that I shouldn't have been the man women trusted to drive them home from the bar or walk them home from the keg party. My love of Tupac might mean that he's just another number of the list of criminals and abusers who I choose to let hold a place in my heart and head.

I have to remind myself that Tupac was only twenty-five when he died. Younger than Jay-Z. Younger than Robert Downey Jr. Only a year older than Dwayne "The Rock" Johnson. Think about how far they've traveled since

1996. When I watch some of those last interviews with Tupac and see his excitement when he talks about future projects and ideas, I see the same spark that's in my students when I ask them what's next after graduation. They light up when they explain how the new internship is going to work out for them. They glow when they imagine stepping out of the car or stepping off a plane in a city where no one knows they share their grandmother's middle name. I see that same spark because Tupac was the same age as the students I'm supposed to lead into a better future for themselves. There's an authenticity I want to believe even though I know Tupac was a good actor. I want to believe he meant it when he spat at those paparazzi. When he says, "That's why I fucked your bitch, you fat motherfucker," at the beginning of "Hit 'Em Up," I want to believe it even though I know there's so much wrong with that opening line.

Of course, youth creates the romantic idea of authenticity. It's easy to imagine Tupac targeting Obama or Bush the way he targeted Clinton and Dole in his lyrics. It's easy to imagine him next to Kanye during the Katrina benefit, jumping in to add his righteous venom right after Kanye says, "George Bush doesn't care about black people." When I watch comic book movies, I think about how Tupac could have been a great supervillain. I can see him spitting a hidden infinity stone out of his cheek just as smoothly as he spit out that razor blade in *Above the Rim*.

But there's also the chance that Tupac at fifty would make me wish that Tupac had died at twenty-five.

There's the chance that Tupac would have been standing next to Kanye in Trump Tower. There's the chance we would have to see Tupac shrug and say, "I respect the hustle," when reporters ask how he could offer this endorsement. There's the chance we'd all have to listen to Tupac say he had questions about jet fuel and steel beams. There's the chance we'd all have to listen to Tupac say his Panther Party upbringing makes him question the vaccines. There's the chance we'd all have to listen to the first three songs of the new Tupac album before we realize, again, that Tupac's new music is never going to touch the same place inside of us that his older music touched back when he was younger and braver and we were younger and braver.

Tupac died when he still had time to be almost anything in life. Now, I'm over a decade older than Tupac ever was. Anniversaries like the anniversary of his death remind us that too many black lives have too many lifetimes stolen from them. But anniversaries like this are recognized by the living, and it's a reminder that I'm lucky to have lived long enough to be something more than an idea to the people who know and love me. There's a world between wondering who I could have been and lamenting that I didn't have more time being who I am. If I'm lucky, I'll make it to being one of those older voices that Tupac railed against. I'll be the C. Delores Tucker that some young firebrand lashes out against because I just don't understand how the world works anymore. If I'm lucky, I'll get to see more young black people carry that same boundless and conflicted energy that Tupac carried when I look across my classroom or look across the living room when I go back to Montgomery for the holidays. And if we're all lucky, that young black energy will have the time it deserves to grow into something sharper and bigger, something more dangerous and more beautiful.

Yeah, Let's Watch It Together.
I'll Wait for You.

**I Keep Saying I'm Never Coming Back
to Kanye but I Keep Coming Back to
His Verse on "Put On"**

No. No. I won't say you're talking crazy because I know what crazy sounds like and crazy is not a sound you'll ever hear fed through a stadium speaker. But no, no. The world doesn't owe you that and it doesn't owe me that, either. But this world does owe me something. For the throats that laughed when I moved my throat to sing. For the tongues that devoured me in the shadows and denied me in the light. For the eyes that saw me as a nigger. For the eyes that saw me as their nigger. For the eyes that saw me as better than the niggers from that other school or that other side of Montgomery. And if I can borrow a second to tell you what this world owes me, then I can borrow all the time this world has ever managed to plunder from the stars to tell you what this world owes the oldest of my name that I can find when liquor and loneliness send me to the ancestry sites. _____ McCall, born in 1817. Born in South Carolina. Born into this world by a woman born in the old world. I won't say his name because I owe him at least that, at least the respect owed to the dead who know they'll never hear the name the gods gave them spoken in this world again. The world owes him a name, and it owes me a name, too, but a part of me too big to hide behind these words is happy to hide behind the bootstraps god I was given because there are things worse than debt. I pray you don't know the feeling of walking by a smile that owes you more than a smile. I pray you never have to shake the hand of a friend who yells, "I ain't forgot you," before they go order another round for the table. Yes, I do pray for you. I pray you can have this loyal spite instead of knowing the feeling of a debt satisfied that doesn't satisfy. I pray you never meet the hollow thrones that are darker and denser than all the possibilities eaten by a black hole. I pray you never know a mountaintop filled with the gods of your grief. I pray you never know what it feels like to claim a diadem of light promised for you and have your debtors throw crumbled signatures at your feet and mumble, "you're welcome." I pray this—I do, I do— but what is a prayer other than another loan bargained on the strength of our backs and knees? And who needs another loan? Who can survive off of the promise of tomorrow when the claws of today and yesterday are claiming their necks?

Inside of You, There Are Two Members of the 1993 New York Knicks. One Knick Is John Starks. One Knick Is Charles Smith

I never dreamed about being a writer when I was younger. I loved words, I guess. I was a second-grade and third-grade spelling bee champion, but it was the competition that motivated me. One of the best feelings of my childhood came from me mouthing, "I got this," to my brother while I stood in line waiting for my chance to defend my title in the third-grade spelling bee in 1993.

I enjoyed the sport of it. Sports were one of my first obsessions. A lot of my personality comes from cheering for the Buffalo Bills while they lost four straight Super Bowls. I probably wouldn't love Hector's last stand in front of the gates of Troy if I didn't watch Scott Norwood's infamous missed field goal in Super Bowl XXV. My favorite college football teams are Alabama and Miami (FL) because the first college game I really remember watching is the 1993 Sugar Bowl. I learned fractions from obsessing over player stats on *Madden* and *NBA Live*. I can forgive a lot of people in life because I had to learn to forgive myself for cheering for North Carolina instead of Michigan in the 1993 NCAA Men's Basketball National Championship.

My relationship with sports influences my relationship with writing in many ways, but it mostly influences how I approach ambition as a writer. I was never the best athlete. Never the fastest. Never the one with the softest hands or the most natural motion. For most of my childhood, I was playing football or basketball in the neighborhood with my older brother, my older cousins, and their friends. I was never the first pick; sometimes, I was only needed to make teams even. But that didn't stop me from getting outside in the summer by 10 a.m. and hoping I didn't have to come home until the sun had set and we could only trust the sound of the ball and the basket to tell us if a shot was made or missed.

I was more of a fighter than an athlete. There were no real fistfights, though there was one postgame sucker punch I haven't forgotten or forgiven after thirty years. I was a fighter on the court because that was the only way to prove I could hang with the other players. I had to prove that I wasn't afraid to take a bump when I jumped to block a shot and wasn't afraid to risk an elbow to the cheek if I crowded a guy on defense. I could hit an open jumper, and I constantly worked on a poor man's version of Larry Bird's behind the backboard baseline shot that he hit against Houston in 1986, but I was never on the court because I could score. If I didn't score at all in a game, I was upset. But if I was the leading scorer in a game, then that meant nobody good was playing in that game.

Sports create connections, and I always connected with teams that reminded me of myself. It's hard for me to get behind flashy teams like the "Showtime" Lakers or the Oregon Ducks football team. I identify most with teams that aren't afraid to be rough and ugly, and the 1992-1993 New York Knicks will always be a special example of that type of team.

I loved the Knicks for a few reasons. I loved hearing the Madison Square Garden crowd chant "DE-FENSE" when the game was close, and I loved hearing the crowd roar even louder when the Knicks got a turnover that led to a fast break. I loved that they weren't afraid to knock an opponent down before they allowed him to score an easy layup or dunk. I loved them because they weren't afraid.

In 1993, every NBA team was supposed to be afraid of the Chicago Bulls because every NBA team was supposed to be afraid of Michael Jordan.

I've never liked Jordan. Even before I knew about his cruel streak or his apocryphal comment about Republicans buying Nikes, I hated Jordan because he looked inevitable. He was too smooth. Too confident. Too good. Even his logo represented a grace I was never going to have.

As a writer, watching Jordan play in the 90s reminds me of reading a Rachel McKibbens poem today. We're both poets; we're both playing the same game. But her work is on a different planet than my work. There's a precision, sharpness, and word economy I'll never touch. There's a talent gap I won't close. And, as a writer, that gap can be demoralizing. That gap can make people stop writing when they run into a talent beyond them, whether that talent is in a book or sitting next to them in a workshop class. That gap can make writers timid. That gap can make writers stop writing.

That gap can also be a challenge. That gap can also be a dare.

In sports, many of the greatest athletes tell stories about how they knew their opponent was defeated before the contest even started. They talk about a look in an opponent's eyes or an opponent's body language that announced defeat before the game started. Even as a young sports fan, I could notice this type of concession when other teams played Jordan and the Bulls. The other teams went through the motions of a basketball game. They high-fived and pumped their fists after a dunk or a made three-pointer. They settled into defensive stances. But it was an act. They didn't believe they could win, and neither did I.

The Knicks didn't act; they believed they could beat Michael Jordan or any other player on the planet, and I was right there believing with them during the 1993 Eastern Conference Finals.

The Knicks had the better regular season record, so Games 1 and 2 were in Madison Square Garden. The Knicks won the first game, but I wasn't too excited. Great teams like the Bulls often gave up early advantages. Opposing teams throw their best shot at a great team early and then run out of steam later in the series. I was happy to see Jordan lose a game, but I was focused on Game 2. If the Knicks won Game 2, I knew even Jordan would have a hard time coming back from a 0-2 deficit in a best-of-seven series.

The Knicks were leading in the fourth quarter of Game 2, but the game was close. With a few minutes left, the Knicks had the ball, and John Starks caught the ball near the baseline. John Starks played the same position as Jordan, and Jordan was defending him in the corner. On top of being the best scorer in the NBA, Jordan was also one of the best defenders due to his determination, athleticism, and competitiveness. There's another apocryphal quote attributed to Michael Jordan. This quote was not directed at Republicans buying Nikes; it was directed at Muggsy Bogues, a fan favorite player who overcame being 5' 3" to have a successful NBA career. In the story, during a game against Jordan in the 1995 playoffs, Bogues had the ball in the fourth quarter and Jordan yelled, "Shoot it you fucking midget." Bogues missed the shot, and, according to the story, that moment shattered Bogues' confidence for the rest of his career. Even during the 1992 Olympics when Jordan was part of the Dream Team, there were stories about him dominating teammates in practice to prove his status as the best player in the world.

John Starks was not the best player in the world.

John Starks was all effort and inconsistency. At his best, he was an energetic defender and dangerous shooter and slasher. At his worst, he was a streaky shooter who didn't know when to stop shooting. The Knicks made it to the NBA finals in 1994, and John Starks' 2/18 shooting performance in Game 7 doomed any hope the Knicks had of beating Houston for the championship that year. To this day, "2/18" is a haunting fraction for Knicks fans.

In the 1993 Eastern Conference Finals, when Starks dribbled down the baseline and saw Jordan and 6' 10" Horace Grant waiting for him, he was supposed to freeze up. He was supposed to throw a bad pass or step out of bounds and give the ball back to the Bulls so they could win the game.

But he didn't freeze. He didn't pass. He drove down the baseline and dunked on Jordan and Grant. That dunk sealed the game for the Knicks, and they took a 2-0 lead against the Bulls.

That game was the last game the Knicks would win in the series. The Bulls won Games 3 and 4 in Chicago, and then another memorable moment happened in Game 5. Game 5 was back in Madison Square Garden, and the Knicks were down by one point with a few seconds left. They got the ball to Charles Smith, their 6' 11" power forward. He was an inch away from the rim. All he had to do was put the ball in the hoop. His first layup was blocked. His second layup was blocked. His third layup was blocked. His fourth layup was blocked, and the Bulls finally got the ball and went down the court to run out the clock for the win.

My friends and I would always talk about the dunks we would do if we were ever gifted with an NBA player's build and skill. We never understood why a player would try a layup when there was a chance to dunk. Layups were a type of disrespect, a thumb in the eye of the god who blessed the player with the ability to dunk. In my life, I've only cared about my height for two reasons: I wanted to be as tall as The Undertaker or Kevin

Nash so that I could step over the ropes of a wrestling ring, and, when I was a teenager, I wished I was an inch taller so that I could have completed one of the hundreds of dunks I missed in my backyard.

In Game 2, John Starks wanted to score a basket, and he jumped over the best player in the world to do it. In Game 5, Charles Smith wanted to score a basket, and he let men six inches shorter than him stand in his way. Both players wanted to complete the same task, but ambition separated them.

Charles Smith got scared, and his team got knocked out of the playoffs. Being scared was the worst sin in my neighborhood. If you didn't get girls, you were a loser who needed to learn how to get some girls. If we thought you were scared of girls, you were a disgrace to our neighborhood and to the responsibility we shared as young boys learning to become men. If you lost a fight, we'd let you know you lost a fight, but we'd remember that you were man enough to fight. If we thought you were scared to fight, we wouldn't accept anything other than an offering of fists, bruises, and blood to prove otherwise.

I think about the Starks play and the Smith play a lot when I think about writing. I don't have the gifts some other writers have. I don't have a natural ear for rhythm. I can't scan a sentence. I don't have a background in other art forms to use for inspiration. I don't have a zip code that makes people think that I'm a great writer.

These shortcomings could mean I should be satisfied with going through the motions of creating art. I could be content to write and teach writing. That would be an acceptable attempt at art in the same way Charles Smith's layups in Game 5 were an acceptable attempt at basketball.

These shortcomings mean that I have a choice. I can choose to submit my work to my dream journals and make them reject me. I can choose to submit my work to publishers I admire and make them reject me. I can choose to write books I'm not good enough to write and see if I can manage to surprise myself and the world.

My ambition led me to one of the biggest surprises of my career. In 2012, I discovered Cornelius Eady was the judge of the annual Marsh Hawk Press Poetry Prize. I was looking for a publisher for my second book of poems. I knew of Cornelius Eady from his position as one of the founders of the Cave Canem organization for black poets and from his own poetry, notably his collection *Brutal Imagination*. I thought it would be great to have one of my poetry idols read my book and reject it. I thought it would have been fun to see him at a conference and know that his eyes touched one of my poems. Even though I knew my odds of winning were a skinny version of slim, I sent in the best book I could write at the time. I didn't have a guarantee that my work would make it out of the slush pile and make it to Eady. I just knew that I had an opportunity in front of me and wanted to see what would happen if I put my whole self into that opportunity. At 5:10 a.m. on July 26, 2012, I received an email titled "Cornelius Eady's decision," and that email told me that he had selected my book as the winner of the 2012 Marsh Hawk Press Poetry Prize.

July 26, 2012, couldn't exist without the game that happened on May 25, 1993. For a night, John Starks was my favorite basketball player. It felt good to see someone take down Jordan. It felt good to watch someone extend himself a little farther than he had a right to. Thirty years later, I'm still looking for ways to push myself and my art into the world, and I'm still looking to prove I'm willing to push and scrap to hold my place on every court.

I Don't Know What To Do About My Obama Shirt

For a good part of my adolescence and adulthood, people knew me for my T-shirts. People wanted to talk to me about the new Marvel or DC movie because there was a good chance I was wearing a Batman or Superman shirt the last time they saw me at a party. My Death Row Records T-shirt has led to some of the most fun conversations I've ever had about music and nostalgia. At undergrad parties, if a pretty girl complimented one of my shirts, I'd say that I let the personality of my T-shirts make up for the personality I didn't have. If she laughed at the joke, I would try another joke and try to see if my humor could take me to a kiss or at least a Facebook friend request. One of my proudest moments in life happened in a Miami strip club when a dancer offered to buy the shirt I was wearing. A dancer in Miami offered me money to take off my clothes. I should have sold her the shirt. That would have made for a better memory. That would have probably made for a better essay.

I've outgrown a lot of those shirts, either physically or mentally. Other shirts got lost during one move or the next. Some have been relegated to holiday shirts appropriate for something like the anniversary of the death of Tupac or The Notorious B. I. G. But, of course, there are still a lot of favorites in the closet that I probably won't wear again but still enjoy seeing in my closet when I'm pushing them to the side to get my Alabama gameday T-shirt or another boring polo shirt to teach in.

These shirts are their own timeline. The black ThunderCats shirt takes me back to Cheap Shots bar the night I met the woman who would become my wife. The yellow Superman shirt takes me back to climbing Mount Olympus during my study abroad trip to Greece. My Obama shirt takes me back to 2008.

It's the Obama shirt that stops me the most when I'm shuffling through my closet.

My favorite day of graduate school at the University of Miami had nothing to do with graduation or nights spent at the TGI Fridays across from campus sharing late night appetizers with my classmates after a seminar that left us wondering why we were giving years of our life to studying poetry or James Joyce.

My favorite day of graduate school happened because Barack Obama happened. It was the day after the 2008 election. I was crossing campus in my Obama shirt that featured a drawing by the legendary comic book illustrator Alex Ross. On the front of the shirt, Obama was opening his shirt to reveal an "O" on his chest and stepping into action in a pose meant to echo Christopher Reeve, the Fleischer cartoons, and all the other versions of Superman I've cheered for in my life. On the way to class. I spotted another student in an

Obama shirt walking my way. We smiled like cousins who hadn't seen each other in five Christmases. We dapped and slapped each other on the back because we were both champions that day. The victory lap carried into my classes. We drank champagne in my poetry workshop, and it might have been the one time we didn't mind the professor's lack of time management making the class run late. This was a party we didn't want to leave early.

The party carried into January 2009 when my mom called me and told she watched the inauguration in the breakroom at JC Penney. She told me she thought about me while she was watching the inauguration. As the last of four children, I never wanted to be a bother. I don't call home as much as I should because I don't want my parents to have to stop what they're doing to answer the phone. Thinking of my mother thinking about me when she watched something that might have seemed impossible to her for most of her life reminded me that I was worth thinking about. The impossible felt a little more possible.

Then the monkey and nigger cartoons popped up, and the party slowed down a bit. Then Ted Kennedy died and universal healthcare died with him. Then the drones kept dropping bombs and the police departments kept dropping black bodies. Then Obama got bullied into showing his papers. Then Obama said the same tired stuff about black fathers. Then Obama played a four-minute offense instead of pushing for the courts or pushing for Kaepernick. Then Obama had to shake Trump's hand and hand over the keys to our future. Then Obama became another president who promised gold and handed us more lead.

With each day since November 4, 2008, it's become easier to pretend we were never fooled into believing the President of the United States could mean something else once a black man managed to be President of the United States. Whenever someone announces they're ending their support for a brand or celebrity, there's always someone in the chorus to announce that they always knew better than to support that brand or celebrity. Someone always knew the NFL was up to no good. Someone never liked R. Kelly in the first place. Someone always boycotted BP and Shell.

In elementary school, I learned the easy role to play was the role of the cynic. The easiest joke to tell was a joke about how some girl really wasn't that pretty or some brainiac really wasn't that smart. When I pretended that nothing impressed me, it was fun to see how much the world would stretch to impress me.

Reading think pieces about how Obama should have known better when he made this decision or that decision makes me think of me and all the other cool kids at the sixth-grade lunch table doing our to best to pretend that nothing in the world was worth our attention.

I'm old enough to know that my sixth-grade game plan was corny, and I think it's corny when critics try to convince us that a black president was no big deal. When my favorite sports teams put a black person in a leadership position, I cheer a little louder. When my country put a black person in a leadership position, I'm not ashamed to say I cheered a little louder for my country. The same people who talk about being afraid to eat in a Cracker Barrel are obsessed with writing about how Obama should have been braver. The people who post the GIF of Bugs Bunny sawing Florida off the map whenever a Southern state passes a regressive law are the same people who swear Obama should've known what America would do after they saw him take the Oath of Office.

But America was America a long time before any of us knew how to pronounce Barack Obama's name. This country had plenty of hate in its veins when people who looked like me and people who looked like Barack Obama were clearing the Carolina swamps and turning the Alabama Black Belt into the most valuable stretch of land on Earth. The country wanted me to be small enough to fit in the hull of a ship with hundreds of people who looked like me, and this country still wants to remind me of how small I am when it asks me to show my ID in the campus parking lot before I go teach in a building named after some Klansmen or eugenicist. This country wants me to forget so many things, and that's why I need reminders like the shirts in my closet. I need to remember that there's something stronger than the sweet and bitter myths that tell me this country has to be this way. I need that Obama shirt to remind me that we thought this world could be better, and, for a little while, we were right. This Obama shirt, and all the other T-shirts in my closet, remind me of so many things I've gained and lost since I packed my first set of luggage and drove to college. They remind me that I get to hold on to some part of the past, some part of myself, even after the world tells me it's time to move on.

When CM Punk Changes His Theme Music, You Must Change Your Life

"Miseria Cantare: The Beginning" (2003-2005)

When the music starts and I see him for the first time, he talks about how he doesn't know if he can survive in a world of conformity, and at the time I'm thinking about if I can survive another trip to the psych ward, so I pick him as a new favorite. We're boys trying to survive with the dull tools men left us with. I'm supposed to give up professional wrestling when I grow up, but I can't give up on anything without giving up on everything. This new millennium didn't give us time travel or postcolonial/post-racial harmony. This new millennium gave us embers. The embers of the towers. The embers growing cool on the altars of the heroes our fathers gave us. I was told to worship Jordan and Hogan. I pledged myself to Iverson and him. When he walks to the ring in basketball shorts and calls himself a savior, I'm reminded of all the times I've looked silly in basketball shorts. I'm reminded of all the times I got the world to believe a lie too big to be anything but the truth. When I see his Pepsi tattoo on one shoulder and Cobra tattoo from *GI Joe* on the other, I see myself walking into a tattoo shop at eighteen with $200 of Applebee's money in my pocket and asking for a phoenix so the world will know that I know I'm never going to escape this spiral of heavens and hells. If he can say he's the best in the world with a straight face and get us to believe it, then I can believe I can be more than a second son from a forgotten part of Montgomery, more than a picture my friends will post on Facebook each year during Suicide Awareness Month. I can believe that it's not about burning out; it's about burning bright enough to make every eye notice.

"This Fire Burns" (2006-2011)

When the music changes, it's 2006 and the new song is a song of destiny. All he needs is a fair shot to show he can shine as bright as anyone. All he needs is for the bosses and the politics to get out of the way. For years, I nod my head while my classmates tell me how to make my poems more like Alabama. I nod my head while I take a break from grading the one hundred essays I brought home over the weekend. I nod my head while I try to remember the email logins for my three part-time jobs. I nod my head while I lie to my girlfriend and my parents when they ask if I need help with the rent. I nod and write more poems. I nod and teach more classes. I nod and move forward until 2011 when he makes it to the big match in Chicago and I make it to my first book deal. Nobody can question if we deserve to be here now. My book goes on sale on my birthday. I celebrate by quitting one of my jobs, and I know what it feels like to be a champion.

"Cult of Personality" (2011-2014)

When the music changes, he can't pretend he's an outsider anymore. His speeches are sponsored by Skittles. He's gone from the face of a revolution to the face of an earnings report. He's Coogler moving from *Fruitvale Station* to *Black Panther*. He's the Alabama Shakes moving from my favorite bar to jewelry store commercials and movie soundtracks. He's every friend who can't come back home for the holidays because their plan was always to leave home and not come back. But I can't pretend I'm an outsider, either. I'm one of the lucky ones. I have a book and a full-time job and a retirement account. When my girlfriend wants to go to St. Louis or Miami, it's not just another daydream on the thrift store couch. I'm busy collecting my own championships. I collect the award from Cornelius Eady. I collect the check when the bartender leaves the tab for me and my friends. I listen to my friends complain about the system and how the system needs to change, but when I order another round without thinking about my bank balance, the system tastes good. But being one of the lucky ones doesn't save him from the injuries he's supposed to ignore. It doesn't save him from losing his cut when the company launches their streaming service. Being lucky isn't enough to keep him from quitting in 2014. And in 2014 I don't want to quit life anymore but I do want to quit my job each time I walk by my book cover that's stuck behind a plant in a dark corner of my department building on campus. My colleagues congratulate me on Monday and then ask if I'm lost when they see me checking my faculty mailbox on Wednesday. But I can't quit because my girlfriend is disabled now and needs insurance now and this is how my girlfriend becomes my wife. I'm a husband now and being a husband is better than being a boyfriend when I need answers from the doctors and lawyers. I collect awards. I collect debt. I collect medical forms I don't know how to complete. I collect $25 every time I give plasma. If professional wrestling has taught me anything, it's how a story is supposed to end. I know I'm going to hit a financial wall or a physical wall or a spiritual wall. I know my wife will end up in the care of someone or somewhere better than me. I know I'll end up back in the corner of my favorite bar where I'll nurse a beer and a scowl. I'll leave home one day and those daydreams about drifting my car across the median will drift into reality.

"Cult of Personality" (2021-)

When he comes back, it's the second year of the pandemic. The music doesn't change, but the world has changed. I've found a job that lets me only have one job. I don't have to share an office, and my wife and I don't have to share combo meals and pretend it's romantic. When he comes back, I'm also trying to find my way back into a world that tried to kill me and nearly succeeded. I'm also trying to remember when to take off my mask and let the world see my smile. I'm also trying to figure out what to do with the gray hair the last few years has left in my beard. When he comes back, we cheer as loud as we can for him, and we cheer even louder for ourselves. We kept going long enough to be here. I know it's all a show, and I know the most important fights are the fights that we'll never see, but I'm still happy to see him bleed one more time. But this time, he's not playing savior and martyr. He's being the friend who invites us out for the weekend to remind us we can still love the mystery that comes with a Friday night. This is the reason I never give up on what I love, and I'm still here watching because I love the memory of watching with my cousin who died at forty and watching with my cousin who died at forty-six and watching with my brother who I only talk to on the holidays and watching with my grandfather who might not remember me and the time he told me Ravishing Rick Rude was the masked man at Halloween Havoc. When the music changes, I know a hero has become a villain. I know the upstart has become the standard. When the music changes, I know the wrestler will swear they never changed, but it was the fans who changed, and I know that will always be true.

When You Choose *Thor: The Dark World* Over *12 Years a Slave*

Tap into your Southern blood and blame Obama. A black president. A black nerd president. Anything is possible. These days, alien-space-Vikings seem as unreal as the Middle Passage.

Be the black man the radio hosts swear you are: Take it out on your girlfriend. You can't deal with her spending Friday night guilty about her freedom, starting every other sentence with "I know I can't relate to them, but…" Apologize for not having a girlfriend who's "down" when you tell the story to your friends back home. Forget that it takes a "down" girlfriend to sit through two hours of Loki jokes and thirteen minutes of closing credits so you can spend the rest of the night giddy over a thirty-second post-credits scene that won't matter until 2017.

Look straight ahead as every other black face turns left while you walk down one more door. Tell yourself it's no different than getting a Classics degree or cheering for the Buffalo Bills. Ready your rebuttals. You paid money to see *Pootie Tang*. You share articles from *The Root*. Sometimes, you used to wake up early enough to watch the last segment of *Melissa Harris-Perry.*

Forgive the premise of a blond god protecting Earth from eternal blackness. Feel good when Idris Elba shows up in the movie. Everyone loves Idris Elba. Think of who wouldn't want to support Idris Elba and start to feel more comfortable in your seat. Watch Idris Elba kill dark-alien-space-elves and remember Paul Mooney's line in *Hollywood Shuffle* about how black actors won't be Rambo until they stop playing Sambo. Idris Elba isn't Rambo, but he's Thor's best black friend. Even the dark-alien-space-elf leader has a best black friend. The black dark-alien-space-elf is just evil; be proud he's not wearing gold chains and dealing dark-alien-space-elf drugs in the alien-space-Viking inner cities. Call that progress.

Think about black dark-alien-space-elves. Are they redundant? Are they extra evil? Do white dark-alien-space-elves let black dark-alien-space-elves play in the elvish basketball league but start locking their doors when two black dark-alien-space-elves move into the neighborhood?

Remember that race lines disappear in a Batman vs. Superman debate. Remind yourself that *Blade* saved the superhero movie genre. Consider the $10 ticket an offering to Wesley Snipes.

Lie. Say you wanted a surprise. *12 Years a Slave* won't throw you a curveball and end up being *17 Years a Slave*. You know that story. You know to keep your credentials close. You know to make sure everyone knows you belong. You heard the stories of your grandfather being called a boy for half his life. You deserve to be here, in this seat, wondering what's so great about

Natalie Portman, wondering how many white faces are in the theater next door.

Tell yourself you thought about supporting the movie, just like your friends who thought about giving blood or thought about joining the service. Tell yourself you'll go next weekend. Blame America when you go next weekend and find out they stopped showing *12 Years a Slave* to make room for *The Hunger Games*. Make a Lenny Kravitz joke and go home.

On the Anniversary of Your Grandmother's Death, You Remember

You remember that you don't understand death now any more than you did when you tried to explain it to your three-year-old niece after she asked if grandmother was coming back. You remember to think of her as "grandmother" even though you always called her "grandma" because you were always good at creating distance. You used to rebound with your elbows out. Your front kick kept the other black belts at bay during Tae Kwon Do tournaments. You'd only say that it was good when the girls asked about it the morning after. You remember every maxim you toss to your students in upper-level workshops. The writer isn't the narrator. Even the truth is its own type of fiction. It's never possible to say exactly what happened.

You know what happened. You hear the banging on the front door. You hear the aunt crying and clawing at the phone on the kitchen wall. You hear your voice relaying the information for the rest of the day. You've been saying, "I think she's dead," for twenty-five years even though you knew she was dead the first time you said those words into the phone. You think about Gilgamesh holding Enkidu's body. You won't think about the rot. You won't acknowledge the skill the country has developed for breaking black women. For once, you wish black women were superhuman. You wish your grandmother was just trying to outdo Jesus. You wish she was just holding her breath until the Romans dropped their guard and she could escape the earth. She'd hate to hear you talking about Jesus this way, but she'd be happy that you were talking about Jesus.

You remember that you took your first creative writing class the year after she died. You remember that you don't believe in coincidence. You remember all the other places you tried to hide after she died. You tried to hide yourself in *Final Fantasy VII*. You tried to hide yourself in puberty. You tried to hide yourself in busboy jobs. You tried to hide yourself in perfect test scores and polyester superhero shirts. You know that using the second person wouldn't fool her. She was probably there the first time you noticed the face in the mirror was your face. She knew your secrets since you learned how to make secrets. She knew your imagination since you learned to imagine on her screened porch and in her dirt patch of a front yard two lots down from the church. She knows who you are. Don't the best teachers tend to remember their students?

You remember that she was your first writing teacher. You still light up whenever you see one of those writing pads with the dotted line down the middle of each row. You make plans every year to buy one to display in your office as a reminder. You never make good on that plan. You can't imagine how many times you had to erase the middle of your alphabet when you got *J* and *K* mixed up, but you do know how good it felt to write a lowercase cursive *f* and have grandmother recognize it as a lowercase cursive *f*. You remember that she didn't let you get away with the excuse of being left-handed. You remember that she didn't let you get away with the excuse of your skin. You remember all the writing teachers that didn't see your sloppy writing and only saw your skin. You remember the writing teachers who didn't correct your sloppy allusions or stale Trojan War metaphors because they were so impressed that you knew about allusions and about the Trojan War. They probably figured your writing was connected to your skin, and since your skin couldn't be corrected, your writing couldn't be corrected, either.

You remember the effort you used to put into your handwriting. You think about all the lessons you've forgotten when you sign the bill for the South Beach dinner that's a world away from your grandmother's hot kitchen where you shared a table with your cousin and the roaches. Grandmother is there when you sign the bill for the deluxe cable package, still there giving you the same warning to get your writing done before you look at the TV. You imagine she's looking over your shoulder when you spread your sloppy signature across the contract for the new book, new apartment, new job. You notice your signature getting worse as your life gets better. Your name fades to a smudge the farther you get from your grandmother's living room. Every now and then, you remember the efforts and blood hiding in your name, and your pride will show in the giant *J* you'll write the next time you have to sign your name. You want to thank her for all of this, but she won't let you. She won't let you go into some big narrative about how the writing lessons you give your students started in her shotgun house on Alexander Street on the west side of Montgomery. She won't allow that, but you imagine she's somewhere proud and waiting to tease her professor grandson about thinking he's too old and too important to give his grandmother a hug.

You remember her skin. The moles. The wrinkles that shouldn't have been there so early in life. You never thought of your grandmother as being too young for her wrinkles until you wrote the previous sentence. You only think about your grandmother's age when you get mad and remind friends, family, lovers, or gods that your grandmother was only fifty-seven. Her skin was bright. She was bright. You remember a story about Indian blood in the family, but you suspect there's a less interesting reason your grandmother lived her life in golden skin. Someone gave her her skin just like someone gave you every last name in your family tree. The color of her skin makes you remember all the girls you fell in love with who had the same skin. Maybe it wasn't colorism that made it so easy for you to fall for golden-brown girls. Maybe your brain sees golden-brown skin and sees your grandmother's love. Maybe you wanted those girls because you wanted someone else to love you like your grandmother loved you. You wrote so many love letters for those girls, so many love letters disguised as poems, disguised as algebra homework, disguised as Facebook small talk. So much love for that skin to make up for not being brave enough to walk into your grandmother's viewing. So much greed to hold that skin in place to make up for how your grandmother slipped away.

You wonder if she still makes time to judge your words. You want her opinion on the suicide note you sent via text in 2005. You want to know if you would have needed to say goodbye to anyone if she had been there in 2005. You want to know if she thinks you're a better poet when you use couplets or tercets. She'd probably tell you to stop acting so smart and call them triplets. She would come to your readings in Montgomery. She wouldn't read your poetry, but she'd always ask what you were writing about when you came home for Thanksgiving and Christmas. She'd always remind you to come home more often.

You see her face in the obituary that your cousin screenshotted for you. You get the screenshot the same week that you watch the HBO documentary on Andre the Giant. You talk to your wife about the grueling nature of professional wrestling. You mansplain how the sport is choreographed but not fake. You talk about how some of the pain is real. You talk about the time Mick Foley's tooth went through his top lip and into his nose at King of the Ring 1998. You talk about Road Warrior Animal getting off a motorcycle the wrong way at SummerSlam 1992 and wrestling a match with his tights seared to his calf. You and your wife wince when the documentary says Andre's organs never stopped growing. His insides were never satisfied with being just the Eighth Wonder of the World. He was hiding agony every time he threw a wrestler across the ring or shrugged off groups of men ganging up on him in a battle royale. You realize Andre was fading long before Hulk Hogan's Atomic Leg Drop at WrestleMania III. You think about Robin Wright being held up by wires because Andre was too weak to hold her in his arms when they filmed *The Princess Bride*. You think about the stories of Andre standing on a box to look even taller. But you're not thinking of Andre. You're thinking of the part in Grandma's obituary that thanked the Alabama Kidney Foundation. You feel dumb for trying to pretend that Grandma was ever "Grandmother." You're thinking about her two decades of transplants and treatments. You see the big smiles and the big hugs every time you left her house. You're thinking about your arms around a corpse. Yes, every body you've ever wrapped your arms around will be a corpse, but this is different. You're thinking about how she might have been the best performer you've ever seen. And part of you is happy that your grandma was hurting every day that you knew her because you hurt every day. Where else did you learn to hide underneath all the puns and punchlines in your poetry? Where else did you learn how to tilt your throat at the right angle to make "I'm dying" sound like "I love you"?

The obituary also tells you that you share her husband's name. You always thought you remembered your aunt telling you that once, but you were always too scared to ask for confirmation. You were scared your name was accidental. You were scared your name didn't belong to the family. You don't know if you want to know more. What happens when a body that became a ghost becomes a body of evidence? You wish your grandma was alive, but you don't know if you want your grandma to be real.

You remember that Grandma is your mother's mother, and you remember that your mother is the oldest of seven and that means your mother has been a mother most of her life. You remember that your mother couldn't think of an answer when you asked her what she dreamed about growing up to be when she was a kid. You never think of your mother as a child unless you are thinking of how it must feel for a child to lose her mother. You remember that your first memory is the feeling of falling asleep to the rhythm of your mother's bobbing knee. You've seen nephews and nieces and a great-niece bobbed to sleep on your mother's knee. You know someone taught her knee that rhythm. You dream about finding a way to talk to your mother about all the things both of you learned from her mother. You wake up and remember the weight of your mother in your arms when she fainted in church the first Sunday after the funeral. You know you're still not strong enough to hold her.

You think about journeys and think about Gilgamesh again and what he did to himself when he finally discovered the word "tomorrow" might come from the old word for blinking and even stars and the stars' favorite children can't blink forever. You remember the saying about not seeking the masters but seeking what they sought. You remember that you don't know what your grandma was seeking. You only know that you will never know what a black woman born in 1940 deserves from this world. You don't know why she was in Illinois when your mother was born. You don't know if it was boldness or fear that brought her back to Alabama. You don't know if you've been writing for twenty-five years to avenge her death or to prove to the same god that took her that your family can't be erased by a god or a government or a kidney failure.

You don't know what your first teacher wanted out of life, but you remember what she wanted out of you. She wanted you to remember that letters were never just lines on paper. She wanted you to know how to spell your name no matter how many other names the world gave you. You won't have a child, so you won't have a grandchild practicing letters in your living room. But you'll always have someone looking over your shoulder. She wanted you to know that your words will always matter to someone. Someone might be a grandma. Someone might be a teacher. Someone might be a student in need of a teacher. Someone might be waiting on you to study their letters, to show them how to make their name bright enough for the most distant stars to see.

All the Thanks

All the thanks in the world to the people who made this book possible. This is my first nonfiction book, so it feels like my debut all over again.

All the thanks to Michael Wheaton and the Autofocus team. You're building something special, and I'm happy this book gets to be a small part of it.

All the thanks to the Alabama State Council on the Arts for supporting this book during its development.

All the thanks to Rebecca Gregory, Jerry Lawrence, Betsy Hogan, MC Hyland, Harry Thomas, Kate Bernheimer, Leah Nielsen, Michael Martone, Ashley McWaters, Paolo Javier, Walter Lew, Mia Leonin, and Maureen Seaton (RIP) for being my writing teachers.

All the thanks to the schools that helped me figure out how to be the nerd I wanted to be: Peter Crump Elementary, Baldwin Magnet Junior High, Booker T. Washington Magnet High, The University of Alabama, and the University of Miami.

All the thanks to the classmates, editors, and friends who've taken the time to see my work and see me.

All the thanks to my big sisters Tonya and Shonda and my big brother Lind for making sure my childhood included *The Last Dragon* and *Rocky III*.

All the thanks to my big brother Lind and my cousins Kevin and Darius (RIP) for the days we spent in the room arguing over who cheated in *Street Fighter II*.

All the thanks to my cousin Kim for all the days we spent at Grandma's house together before we were old enough to go to school.

All the thanks to Cammy and Brian for showing me all the parts of myself I could bring to nonfiction.

All the thanks to Kiese Laymon, Ashley M. Jones, Jason Mott, Tiana Clark, and all the other great black writers who are writing great work about the South. My work wouldn't exist without your work.

All the thanks to my grandfather Daniel McCall and my grandmother Ida McCall for feeding me desserts and letting me watch wrestling pay-per-views at their house.

All the thanks to my grandmother Ethel Ophelia Washington for the hugs I can still feel. Your name is in a book. How hard would you hug me for putting your name in a book?

All the thanks to my parents Lindsey and Ethel for letting me scribble at the dining room table and never doubting those scribbles could grow up to be this.

All the thanks to Sara for being a wife willing to sit with me through so many hours of bad wrestling and bad superhero movies. All the thanks to Sara for being willing to sit with me.

All the thanks to me. You're still here. It's okay to be happy about it.

Acknowledgements

Thankful acknowledgement is given to the following journals in which the essays listed below first appeared:

Autofocus: "We Hate *Wonder Woman 1984* Because Nobody Ever Granted Our Wish" and "I Keep Saying I'm Never Coming Back to Kanye but I Keep Coming Back to His Verse on 'Put On'" (Published as "I Keep Telling Myself I'm Done with Kanye but I Keep Remembering His Verse on 'Put On'")

Lunch Ticket: "When You Choose *Thor: The Dark World* Over *12 Years a Slave*"

Nat. Brut: "*Tha Carter V* Means the South's Not Dead, Either"

Pleiades: "Watching Tennis Is the Whitest Thing I'll Ever Be Allowed To Do" and "When CM Punk Changes His Theme Music, You Must Change Your Life"

Quarterly West: "The New Transported Man" (Published as "5,000 Days")

The Rumpus: "Oscar Grant's America"

The Under Review: "824 Words" and "My Dad Still Watches the NFL"

Variant Literature: "It Doesn't Feel Like Tupac's Been Dead for 25 Years Because Sometimes It Doesn't Feel Like Tupac Is Dead"

About the Author

Jason McCall is the author of the essay collection *Razed by TV Sets* and the poetry collections *What Shot Did You Ever Take* (co-written with Brian Oliu); *A Man Ain't Nothin'*; *Two-Face God*; *Mother, Less Child* (co-winner of the 2013 Paper Nautilus Vella Chapbook Prize); *Dear Hero*, (winner of the 2012 Marsh Hawk Press Poetry Prize and co-winner of the 2013 Etchings Press Whirling Prize); *I Can Explain*; and *Silver*. He and P.J. Williams are the editors of *It Was Written: Poetry Inspired by Hip-Hop*. He holds an MFA from the University of Miami. He is a native of Montgomery, Alabama, and he currently teaches at the University of North Alabama.

⌈a⌉
— also from Autofocus Books —

Duplex — Mike Nagel

XO — Sara Rauch

Until It Feels Right — Emily Costa

Cleave — Holly Pelesky

Nextdoor in Colonialtown — Ryan Rivas

Too Much Tongue — Adrienne Marie Barrios & Leigh Chadwick

Picture Window — Danny Caine

the nature machine! — Tyler Gillespie

A Kind of In-Between — Aaron Burch

How to Write a Novel: An Anthology of 20 Craft Essays About Writing, None of Which Ever Mention Writing — ed. Aaron Burch

Hiraeth — Mistie Watkins

That Spell — Tate N. Oquendo

My Modest Blindness — Russell Brakefield

A Calendar Is A Snakeskin — Kristine Langley Mahler

Culdesac — Mike Nagel

Printed in the USA
CPSIA information can be obtained
at www.ICGtesting.com
CBHW020816290224
4693CB00005B/14